- Biography Series -

Nobel Laureates

By

Archana Srinivasan

FIRST EDITION

An imprint of Sura Books (Pvt) Ltd.
(An ISO 9001 : 2000 Certified Company)
Chennai ● Tirunelveli ● Ernakulam ● Palakkad
● Thiruvananthapuram ● Bengalooru

Price: ₹40.00

© PUBLISHERS

NOBEL LAUREATES

By

Archana Srinivasan

This Edition : October, 2011
Size : 1/8 Demy
Pages : 96
Code : BI 13

Price: ₹40.00

ISBN : 81-7478-589-2

FIRST EDITION

[An imprint of Sura Books (Pvt) Ltd.]

Head Office: 1620, 'J' Block, 16th Main Road, Anna Nagar,
Chennai - 600 040. Phones: 044-26162173, 26161099

Branches : • KAP Complex, I Floor, 20, Trivandrum Road,
Tirunelveli - 627 002. Phone : 0462-4200557

• XXXII/2328, New Kalavath Road,
.Opp. to BSNL, Near Chennoth Glass, Palarivattom,
Ernakulam - 682 025. Phones: 0484-3205797, 2535636

• Shop No. 7, Municipal Complex, Robinson Road,
Palakkad - 678 001. Phone : 0491-2504270

• TC 28/2816, Sriniketan, Kuthiravattam Road, Chirakulam,
Thiruvananthapuram - 695 001. Phone: 0471-4063864

• 3638/A, IVth Cross, Opp. to Malleswaram Railway Station,
Gayathri Nagar, Back gate of Subramaniya Nagar,
Bengalooru - 560 021. Phone: 080-23324950

Printed at Novena Offset Printing Co., Chennai - 600 005 and Published by
V.V.K.Subburaj for First Edition [An imprint of Sura Books (Pvt) Ltd.]
1620, 'J' Block, 16th Main Road, Anna Nagar, Chennai - 600 040.
Phones: 044-26162173, 26161099. Fax: (91) 44-26162173.
email: enquiry@surabooks.com; website: www.surabooks.com

10 11 1000

Contents

BIOGRAPHY SERIES

Nobel Laureates

Albert Camus

Albert Camus, French novelist, essayist and playwright, received the 1957 Nobel Prize for literature. Camus was closely linked to his fellow existentialist Jean-Paul Sartre in the 1940s, but he broke with him over Sartre's support to Stalinist politics. Camus died in a car accident near Sens, France, on January 4, 1960. Among his best-known novels are *The Stranger* and *The Plague*.

> *"Mother died today. Or maybe yesterday, I don't know. I had a telegram from home: 'Mother passed away. Funeral tomorrow. Yours sincerely.' That doesn't mean anything. It may have happened yesterday."* (from The Stranger)

Albert Camus was born in Mondovi, Algeria, in a working-class family. His mother was an illiterate charwoman and father an itinerant agricultural laborer, who was killed in World War I in the Battle of Marne. Camus's mother was shocked by the news of her husband's death, and she suffered a stroke that permanently impaired her speech. In 1923, Camus won a scholarship to lycée in Algiers, where he studied from 1924 to 1932. Incipient tuberculosis put an end to his athletic activities, and the disease troubled Camus for the rest of his life. Between the years 1935 and 1939 Camus held various jobs in Algiers, and he also joined the Communist Party.

In 1936, Camus received his *diplôme d'étudies supérieures* from the University of Algiers in philosophy, and to recover his health he made his first visit to Europe. Camus's first book L'ENVERS ET L'ENDROIT, a collection of essays, appeared in 1937.

By this time Camus's reputation in Algeria as a leading writer was growing. He was also active in theatre. In 1938, Camus moved to France, and divorced next year his first wife, Simone Hié, who was a morphine addict. From 1938 to 1940 Camus worked for the *Alger-Républicain* and in 1940, for *Paris-Soir*. He married Francine Faure in 1940 and taught in Oran, Algeria, in 1942.

During World War II, Camus was a member of the French resistance. He was a reader and editor of Espoir series at Gallimard publisher from 1943 and founded with Sartre the left-wing newspaper *Combat*, serving as its editor. His second novel, L'ÉTRANGER (The Stranger), which he had begun in Algeria before the war, appeared in 1942. It has been considered one of the greatest of all hard-boiled novels. Camus admired the American tough novel and wrote in *The Rebel* (1951) that **"it does not choose feelings or passions to give a detailed description of, such as we find in classic French novels. It rejects analysis and the search for a fundamental psychological motive that could explain and recapitulate the behavior of a character..."** The story is narrated by a doomed character, Mersault, and is set between two deaths, his mother's and his own. Mersault is a clerk, who seems to have no feelings and spends afternoons in love-making and empty nights in the cinema. He reaches self-knowledge by committing a crime – he shoots an Arab on the beach without explicit reason and motivation - it was hot, the Arab had earlier terrorized him and his friend Raymond, and he had a headache. Mersault is condemned to die as much for his refusal to accept the standards of social behavior as for the crime itself. In the cell Mersault faces the reality for the first time, and his consciousness awakens. **"It was as if that great rush of anger had washed me clean, emptied me of hope, and gazing up at the dark sky spangled with its signs and stars. For the first time, I laid my heart open to the benign indifference of the universe."** Luchino Visconti's film version in 1967 meticulously reconstructed an Algiers street so that it looked exactly as it had during 1938-39, where the story took place. But the 43-year-old Marcello Mastroianni, who played 30-year-old Mesault, was considered too old, although otherwise his performance was praised.

In 1942, appeared Camus's philosophical essay LE MYTHE DE SISYPHE. It starts with the famous statement: **"There is only one really serious philosophical question, and that is suicide. Deciding whether or not life is worth living is to answer the fundamental question in philosophy. All other questions follow from that."** Camus compares the absurdity of existence of humanity to the labours of the mythical character Sisyphus, who was condemned through all eternity to push a boulder to the top of a hill and watch helplessly as it rolled down again. Camus takes the non-existence of God granted and finds meaning in the struggle itself.

"A novel is never anything but a philosophy put into images," Camus wrote. He admired Sartre's gift as a novelist, but did not find his two sides, philosophy and story-telling, equally convincing. In an essay written in 1952, he praises Melville's *Billy Budd*. Melville, according to Camus, "never cut himself off from flesh or nature, which are barely perceptible in Kafka's work." Camus also admired William Faulkner and made a dramatic adaptation of Faulkner's *Requiem for a Nun*.

In 1947 Camus resigned from *Combat* and published in the same year his third novel, LA PESTE, an allegory to the Nazi occupation of France. A small town is abruptly forced to live within narrow boundaries under terror - death is loose on the streets. In the besieged city some people try to act morally, some as cowards, some lovers. **"None the less, he knew that the tale he had to tell could be one of a final victory. It could only be the record of what had to be done, and what assuredly would have to be done again in the never-ending fight against terror and its relentless onslaughts, despite their personal afflictions, by all who, while unable to be saints but refusing to bow down to pestilences, strive their utmost to be healers."**

After his break with Sartre, Camus wrote L'HOMME RÉVOLTÉ, which appeared in 1951. It explores the theories and forms of humanity's revolt against authority. From 1955 to 1956 Camus worked as a journalist for *L'Express*. Among his major works in the late-1950s are LA CHUTE (1956), an ironic novel in which the penitent judge Jean-Baptiste Clamence confesses his own moral crimes to a stranger in an Amsterdam bar. Jean-Baptiste reveals his hypocrisy, but at the same time his monologue becomes an attack on modern man.

At the time of his death, Camus was planning to direct a theatre company of his own and to write a major novel about growing up in Algeria. Several of the short stories in L'EXILE ET LA ROYAUME (1957) were set in Algeria's coastal towns and in hospitable sands, in which the desert is seen as a symbol of void in a soul. The unfinished novel LA MORT HEUREUSE (1970) was written in 1936-38. It presented the young Camus, or Patrice Mersault, seeking his happiness from Prague to his hometown in Algiers, announcing towards the end of the book **"What matters - all that matters, really - is the will to** happiness, a kind of enormous, ever-present consciousness. The rest - women, art, success - is nothing but excuses." In LE PREMIER HOMME (1994), Camus charted the history of his family and his lycée years. The manuscript was found in the car in which he died.

> *"The absurd man will not commit suicide; he wants to live, without relinquishing any of his certainty, without a future, without hope, without illusions, and without resignation either. He stares at death with passionate attention and this fascination liberates him. He experiences the "divine irresponsibility of the condemned man."* (from Sartre Analysis of Mersault, the protagonist of The Stranger, in Literary and Philosophical Essays, 1943) - *"It is not rebellion itself which is noble but the demands it makes upon us."* (from The Plague, 1947)

T. S. Eliot

Thomas Stearns Eliot is an American-English poet, playwright, and literary critic, a leader of the modernist movement in literature. Eliot was awarded the Nobel Prize for literature in 1948. His most famous work is THE WASTE LAND, which was written when he was 34. On one level it describes cultural and spiritual crisis, reflected in its use of fragmentation and discontinuity.

"The point of view which I am struggling to attack is perhaps related to the metaphysical theory of the substantial unity of the soul: for my meaning is, that the poet has, not a 'personality' to express, but a particular medium, which is only a medium and not a personality, in which impressions and experiences combine in peculiar and unexpected ways." (from 'Tradition and the Individual Talent,' 1920)

Thomas Stearns Eliot was born in St. Louis, Missouri, the seventh and youngest child of a distinguished family of New England origin. His forebears included the Reverend William Greenleaf Eliot, founder of Washington University in St. Louis, and on his mother's side, Isaac Stearns, one of the original settlers of Massachusetts Bay Colony. Eliot's father was a prosperous industrialist and his mother wrote among others a biography of William Greenleaf Eliot.

Eliot was educated at Smith Academy in St. Louis and Milton Academy in Massachusetts. He graduated from Harvard, where he contributed poetry to *Harvard Advocate*. He spent a year in France, attending lectures at the Sorbonne. After Eliot returned to Harvard, he completed a dissertation on the English idealist philosopher F.H. Bradley, and studied Sanskrit and Buddhism.

In 1914, he moved into England and started to reform poetic diction with Ezra Pound, who was largely responsible for getting Eliot's early poems into print - among them THE LOVE SONG OF J. ALFRED PRUFROCK in the Chicago magazine *Poetry* in 1915. The title character is tormented by the difficulty of articulating his complex feelings. Prufrock is a perfect gentleman and tragic in his conventionality. He has heard "the mermaids singing" but is paralyzed by self-consciousness - "I do not think that they will sing to me." Denis Donoghue has pointed out in *Words Alone* (2000) that in his early poems, Eliot did not start with a theme but with a fragment of rhythm or motif. Prufrock has not the qualities of a person, he is a fragmented voice with a name. **"Eliot's language here and in the early poems generally refers to things and simultaneously works free from the reference. He seems always to be saying: "That is not what I meant at all. / That is not it, at all." When he gives a voice a name—Prufrock, Gerontion—he makes no commitment beyond the naming."** (from *Words Alone*)

Pound also introduced Eliot to Harriet Weaver, who published Eliot's first volume of verse, PRUFROCK AND OTHER OBSERVATIONS, in 1917. Eliot taught for a year at Highgate Junior School in London, and then worked as a clerk at Lloyds Bank. A physical condition prevented his entering in 1918 into the US Navy. In 1919 appeared Eliot's second book, ARA VOS PREC (published in the U.S. as POEMS), hand-printed by Virginia and Leonard Woolf at the Hogath Press.

In an early essay, 'Tradition and the Individual Talent' (1919) Eliot propounded the doctrine that poetry should be impersonal and free itself from Romantic practices. **"The progress of an artist is a continual self-sacrifice, a continual extinction of personality."** Eliot sees in this depersonalization that art approaches science. With his collection of essays, THE SACRED

WOOD (1920), and later published THE USE OF POETRY AND THE USE OF CRITICISM (1933) and THE CLASSICS AND THE MAN OF LETTERS (1942), Eliot established his reputation as a critic and had an enormous impact on contemporary literary taste. In 1922 Eliot founded the *Criterion*, a quarterly review that he edited until he halted its publication at the beginning of World War II. In 1925, he joined the publishing house of Faber and Gwyer (later Faber and Faber), becoming eventually one of the firm's directors. Between the years 1917 and 1919, Eliot was an assistant editor of the journal the *Egoist* and from 1919 onwards he was a regular contributor to the *Times Literary Supplement*.

In the 60 years from 1905 to his death, Eliot published about 600 articles and reviews. Eliot's principle purpose in his literary-critical essays was **"the elucidation of works of art and the correction of taste."** He wanted to revive the appreciation of the 17th-century "Metaphysical poets," referring to such writers as Donne, Crashaw, Vaughan, Lord Herbert and Cowley. He admitted that it is extremely difficult to define metaphysical poetry and decide what poets practiced but praised the complex mixture of intellect and passion that characterized their work. In the essay 'Religion and literature' (1935) Eliot stated that **"literary criticism should be completed by criticism from a definite ethical and theological standpoint."**

Eliot's first marriage in 1915 with the ballet-dancer Vivienne Haigh-Wood turned out to be unhappy. She was temperamental, full of life and restless. Her arrival at menstruation brought extreme mood swings, pains and cramps; her condition was diagnosed as hysteria. From 1930 until her death in 1947 she was confined in mental institutions. Later Eliot married his secretary, Valerie Fletcher. Carole Seymour-Jones has argued in *Painted Shadow: A Life of Vivienne Eliot* (2001) that Eliot's sexual orientation was fundamentally gay.

Eliot avoided sharing bed with Vivienne, who started an affair with Bertrand Russell. Virginia Woolf once said: "He was one of those poets who lived by scratching, and his wife was his itch."

The appearance of *The Waste Land* (1922), a poetic exploration of the soul - or civilization's struggle for regeneration, made Eliot world famous. Following Pound's suggestion, Eliot reduced *The Waste Land* to about half its original length. The first version, with Pound's revisions, was published in 1971. The long poem caught the mood of confusion after World War I, when everything in society seemed to be changing and and many felt that pre-war values were lost.

Divided into five sections, *The Waste Land* is a series of fragmentary dramatic monologues, a dense chorus of voices and culture historical quotations, that fade on into another. Moreover, Eliot didn't hesitate to combine slang with scholarly language. The Waste Land is an image of Spenglerian magnitude, is contrasted with sources of regeneration, such as fertility rituals and Christian and Eastern religious practices. For the work, Eliot drew materials from several sources, among them were the Grail story, the legend of the Fisher King, Sir James George Frazer's *Golden Bough*, and Dante's *Commedia*, but when Dante finally reunit with Beatrice in 'Heaven', *The Waste Land* ends ambiguously with a few words of Sanskrit. In a way the work fulfilled Eliot's "impersonal theory of poetry": **"The poet's mind is infact a receptacle for seizing and storing up numberless feelings, phrases, images, which remain there until all the particles can unite to from a new compound which are present together."**

In 1927, Eliot became a British citizen and member of the Church of England. His pilgrimage towards his own particular brand of High Anglicanism may be charted in his poetry, starting from 'The Hollow Men' (1925) to visions in FOUR QUARTETS (135-42), consisting of 'Burnt Norton', 'East Cocer', The Dry Salvages', and 'Little Gidding,' into which he integrated his experiences in World War II as a watchman checking for fires during bombing raids. These quartets represent the four seasons and four elements. Helen Gardner has described the whole work as an '**austere and rigorously philosophic poem on time and time's losses and gains.**' (*The Composition of Four Quarters*, 1978)

Eliot's other works include poetic dramas, in which his dramatic verse became gradually indistinguishable from prose. MURDER IN THE CATHEDRAL (1935) was written for a church performance and treated the martyrdom of St. Thomas Beckett. In THE FAMILY REUNION (1939) Eliot took to the theme of contemporary life, and tried to find a rhythm close to contemporary speech. THE COCTAIL PARTY (1950) was partly based on *Alcestis* of Euripides. Eliot took in it greater liberties with ordinary colloquial speech.

> *"What we have to do is to bring poetry into the world in which the audience lives and to which it returns when it leaves the theatre; not to transport the audience into some imaginary world totally unlike their own, an unreal world in which poetry can be spoken. What I should hope might achieved, by a generation of dramatists having the benefit of our experience, is that the audience should find, at the moment of awareness that it is hearing poetry, that it is saying to itself: "I could talk in poetry too!" Then we should not be transported into an artificial world; on the contrary, our own sordid, dreary, daily world would be suddenly illuminated and transfigured."*
> *(from* Poetry and Drama, *1951)*

Eliot was an incurable joker and among his many pranks was to seat visiting authors in chairs with whoopee cushions and offer them exploding cigars. To the poet's pleasure, the American comedian Groucho Marx was his great fan. In 1964, he wrote to Groucho: **"The picture of you in the newspaper** saying that, amongst other reasons, you have come to London to see me has greatly enchanted my credit line in the neighborhood, and particularly with the greengrocer across the street." OLD POSSUM'S BOOK OF PRACTICAL CATS (1939), Eliot's classical book of verse for children, has achieved a considerable world success in a musical adaptation. His most influential exercise in social criticism was NOTES TOWARD A DEFINITION OF CULTURE (1948).

Eliot died in London on January 4, 1965. His fame has been shadowed by accusations of racism, misogynism, fascism, emotional coldness, and anti-semitism, which has made him unpleasant for many readers. However, he has not been regarded as a Communist. Hints of Eliot's anti-semitism, like in the poem 'Burbank With a Baedeker: Bleistein With a Cigar,' has been considered a questionable outgrowth of his theology, or due to a class prejudice, but never the center of his thought. The poem's reputation, however, is notorious, but the possibility that Eliot perhaps was parodying anti-semitism or made a statement on misreading Dante, also offers an alternative way of reading it. (see Patricia Sloane's work *T.S. Eliot's Bleistein Poems*, 2000)

> *For Thine is*
> *Life is*
> *For Thine is the*
>
> *This is the way the world ends*
> *This is the way the world ends*
> *This is the way the world ends*
> *Not with a bang but a whimper*
>
> *(from* The Hollow Men*)*

Ernest Hemingway

Hemingway is a famous American novelist, short-story writer and essayist. His deceptively simple prose style has influenced wide range of writers. Hemingway was awarded the 1954 Nobel Prize for Literature. He was unable to attend the award ceremony in Stockholm, because he was recuperating from injuries sustained in an airplane crash while hunting in Uganda.

"Certainly there is no hunting like the hunting of man and those who have hunted armed men long enough and liked it, never really care for anything else thereafter. You will meet them doing various things with resolve, but their interest rarely holds because after the other thing ordinary life is as flat as the taste of wine when the taste buds have been burned off your tongue." (from 'On the Blue Water' in Esquire, *April 1936)*

Ernest Hemingway was born in Oak Park, Illinois. His mother Grace Hall had an operatic career before marrying Dr. Clarence Edmonds Hemingway, who taught his son to love out-door life. Hemingway's father took his own life in 1928 after losing his health to diabetes and his money in the Florida real-estate bubble. Hemingway attended the public schools in Oak Park and published his earliest stories and poems in his high school newspaper. Upon his graduation in 1917, Hemingway worked six months as a reporter for *The Kansas City Star.* He then joined as a volunteer for an ambulance unit in Italy during World War I. In 1918, he suffered a severe leg wound and was twice decorated by the Italian government. His affair with an American nurse, Agnes von Kurowsky, gave basis for the novel A FAREWELL TO ARMS (1929). The tragic love story was filmed first time in 1932, starring Gary Cooper, Helen Hayes, and Adolphe Menjou. In the second version from 1957, written by Ben Hecht and directed by Charles Vidor, Rock Hudson and Jennifer Jones were in the leading roles. Its failure caused David O. Selznick to produce no more films.

After the war, Hemingway worked for a short time as a journalist in Chicago. He moved in 1921 to Paris, where he wrote articles for the *Toronto Star.* "If you are lucky enough to have lived in Paris as a young man, then wherever you go for the rest of your life, it stays with you, for Paris is a moveable feast." (from *A Moveable Feast*, 1964) In Europe, Hemingway associated with writers such as Gertrude Stein and F. Scott Fitzgerald, who edited some of his texts and acted as his agent. Later Hemingway portrayed Fitzgerald in A MOVEABLE FEAST (1964), but not in a friendly light. Fitzgerald, however, regretted their lost friendship. Of Gertrude Stein, Hemingway wrote to Maxwell Perkins, his editor: "She lost all sense of taste when she had menopause. It was really an extraordinary business. Suddenly she couldn't tell a good picture from a bad one, a good writer from a bad one, it all went awry." (from *The Only Thing That Counts*, 1996) When he was not writing for the newspaper or for himself, Hemingway toured with his wife, former Elisabeth Hadley Richardson, in France, Switzerland, and Italy. In 1922, he went to Greece and Turkey to report on the war between those countries. In 1923, Hemingway made two trips to Spain. On the second trip he went to see bullfights at Pamplona's annual festival.

Hemingway's first books, THREE STORIES AND TEN POEMS (1923) and IN OUR TIME (1924), were published in Paris. THE TORRENTS OF SPRING appeared in 1926 and Hemingway's first serious novel, THE SUN ALSO RISES, on the same year. The novel deals with a group of expatriates in

France and Spain, who are members of the disillusioned post-World War I Lost Generation. Main characters are Lady Brett Ashley and Jake Barnes. Lady Brett loves Jake, who has been wounded in war and cannot answer her needs. Although Hemingway never explicitly detailed Jake's injury, is seen that he has lost his testicles but not his penis. Jake and Brett and their odd group of friends have various adventures around Europe, in Madrid, Paris and Pampalona. In an attempt to cope with their despair they turn to alcohol, violence and sex. The story is narrated in first person. As Jake, Hemingway was wounded in World War I. They share also interest in bullfighting. The story ends bitter-sweet: "Oh, Jake, Brett said, "we could have had such a damned good time together." Hemingway wrote and rewrote the novel in various parts of Spain and France between 1924 and 1926. It became his first great success as a novelist. Although the novel's language is simple, Hemingway used understatement and omission which made the text multi-layered and rich in allusions. In 1957 the story was adapted into screen. The film was directed by Henry King, starring Tyrone Power and Ava Gardner.

After the publication of MEN WITHOUT WOMEN (1927), Hemingway returned to the United States, settling in Key West, Florida. Hemingway and Hadley divorced in 1927 and the same year he married Pauline Pfeiffer, a fashion editor. In Florida he wrote *A Farewell to Arms*, which was published in 1929. The scene of the story is the Italian front in World War I, where two lovers find brief happiness. The novel gained enormous critical and commercial success.

In 1930s Hemingway wrote such major works as DEATH IN THE AFTERNOON (1932), a nonfiction account of Spanish bullfighting, and THE GREEN HILL OF AFRICA (1935), a story of a hunting safari in East Africa. "All modern American literature comes from one book by Mark Twain called *Huckleberry Finn*", which is perhaps the most quoted line from the story. TO HAVE AND HAVE NOT (1937) was made into a film by the director Howard Hawks. They had became friends in the late 1930s. Hawks also liked to hunt, fish, and drink, and the author got along with Hawk's wife Slim, who later said: "There was an immediate and instant attraction between us, unstated but very, very strong." According to a story, Hawks had told Hemingway that he can make "a movie out of the worst thing you ever wrote." The author has asked, "What's the worst thing I ever wrote?" and Hawks said, "That piece of junk called *To Have and Have Not.*" "I needed the money," Hemingway said. The screenplay of the film was written by Jules Furthman and William Faulkner.

> *"And then it just occurred to him that he was going to die. It came with a rush, not as a rush of water nor of wind; but of a sudden evil-smelling emptiness, and the odd thing was that the hyena slipped lightly along the edge of it."* (from 'The Snows of Kilimanjaro')

Wallace Stevens once termed Hemingway, "the most significant of living poets, so far as the subject of extraordinary reality is concerned." By 'poet' Stevens referred to Hemingway's stylistic achievements in his short stories. Among his most famous stories is 'The Snows of Kilimanjaro,' which begins with an epitaph telling that the western summit of the mountain is called the House of God, and close to it was found the carcass of a leopard. Down on the savanna the failed writer Harry is dying of gangrene in an hunting camp. "He had loved too much, demanded too much, and he wrote it all out." Just before the end of the story Harry has a vision. He dreams that he is taken up to see the top of Kilimanjaro on a rescue plane - "great, high, and unbelievably white in the sun."

In 1937, Hemingway observed the Spanish Civil war firsthand. As many writers, he supported the cause of the Loyalist. In Madrid he met Martha Gellhorn, a writer and war correspondent, who became his third wife in 1940. In TO WHOM THE BELLS TOLL (1940) Hemingway returned again to Spain. He dedicated his book to Gellhorn - Maria in the story was partly modelled after her. "Her hair was golden brown of a grain field," Hemingway wrote of his heroine. The story covered only a few days and concerned the blowing up of a bridge by a small group of partisans. When the heroine in *A Farewell to Arms* dies at the end of the story after giving birth to a stillborn child, it is time for the hero, Robert Jordan, to sacricife his life for comradeship and love. The theme of the coming of death was also central in the novel ACROSS THE RIVER AND INTO THE TREES (1950).

In addition to hunting expeditions in Africa and Wyoming, Hemingway developed a passion for deep-sea fishing in the waters off Key West, the Bahamas, and Cuba. He also armed his fishing boat, the *Pilar*, and monitored with his crew Nazi activities and their submarines in that area during World War II. In 1940 Hemingway bought Finca Vigia, a house outside Havana, Cuba. Its surroundings were a paradise for his undisciplined bunch of cats. The first years of his marriage with Gellhorn were happy, but he soon realized that she was not a housewife, but an ambitious journalist. Gellhorn called Hemingway her "Unwilling Companion". She was eager to travel and "take the pulse of the nation" or the world. In early 1941 Gellhorn made with Hemingway a long, 30,000 mile journey to China. Just before the Invasion of Normandy in 1944, Hemingway managed to get to London, where he settled at the Dorchester Hotel. Before this he had taken Gellhorn's position as *Collier's* leading correspondent. She arrived two weeks later, and took a separate room. Hemingway observed the D-Day landing below the Normandy cliffs; Gellhorn went ashore with the troops. Back in Paris after many years, Hemingway spent much time at the Ritz Hotel. Hemingways's divorce from Gellhorn in 1945 was bitter. Later Gellhorn said that having "lived with a mythomaniac, I know they believe everything they say, they are not conscious liars, they invent to increase everything about themselves and their lives and *believe* it." In 1946 Hemingway returned to Cuba. After Gellhorn had left him, he married Mary Welsh, a correspondent for *Time* magazine, whom he had met in a London restaurant in 1944.

Hemingway's drinking had started already when he was a reporter. He tolerate large amounts of alcohol and it did not affect the quality of his writing for a long time. In the late 1940s he started to hear voices in his head. He was overweight and the blood pressure was high. His ignorance of the dangers of liquor revealed when he taught his son Patrick to drink, when he was only 12-years old. The same happened with his brothers. Patrick had later in life problems with alcohol. Gregory, who was a transvestite, used drugs - he died at the age of 69 in a women's prison in Florida. After weeks of heavy drinking in Spain, Hemingway went to a doctor, who noted that the author already had clear signs of cirrhosis.

Across the River and Into the Trees was Hemingway's first novel in a decade which was poorly received. THE OLD MAN AND THE SEA, published first in *Life* magazine in 1952, restored again his fame. The 27,000 word novella told a story of an old Cuban fisherman named Santiago, who finally catches a giant marlin after weeks of not catching anything. As he returns to the harbour, the sharks eat the fish, lashed to his boat. The model for Santiago was a Cuban fisherman, Gregorio Fuentes, who died in January 2002, at the age of 104. Fuentes had served as the captain of Hemingway's boat *Pilar* in the late 1930s and was occasionally his tapster. Hemingway also made a fishing trip to Peru in part to shoot footage for a film version of the *Old Man and the Sea*. In 1959 he visited Spain, where he met the famous bullfighter Luis Miguel Dominquín at a hospital. A bull had caught Dominquín in the groin. "Why the hell do the good and brave have to die before everyone else?" he said.

However, Dominquín did not die. Hemingway planned to wrote another book of bullfighting but published instead *A Moveable Feast*, a memoir of the 1920s in Paris.

Much of his time Hemingway spent in Cuba until Fidel Castro's 1959 revolution. He supported Castro but when the living became too difficult, he moved to the United States. When visiting Africa in 1954, Hemingway was in two flying accidents and was taken to a hospital. In the same year he started to write TRUE AT FIRST LIGHT, which was his last full-length book. Part of it appeared in *Sports Illustrated* in 1972 under the title *African Journal*.

In 1960 Hemingway was hospitalized at the Mayo Clinic in Rochester, Minnesota, for treatment of depression, and was released in 1961. During this time he was given electric shock therapy for two months. On July 2 Hemingway committed suicide with his favorite shotgun at his home in Ketchum, Idaho. Several of Hemingway's novels have been published posthumously. *True at First Light*, depiction of a safari in Kenya, appeared in July 1999. It is one of the worst books published by a Nobel writer.

Thomas Mann

Thomas Mann is a German essayist, cultural critic, and novelist, who was awarded the Nobel Prize for Literature in 1929. Among Mann's most famous works is BUDDENBROOKS (1901), which appeared when he was 26. He began writing it during a one-year stay in Italy and completed it in about two and a half years. The book outraged the citizens of Lübeck who saw it as a thinly veiled account of local incidents and figures.

"Regarded as a whole, Mann's career is a striking example of the "repeated puberty" which Goethe thought characteristic of the genius, in technique as well as in thought, he experienced far more daringly than is generally realized. In Buddenbrooks he wrote one of the last of the great "old-fashioned" novels, a patient, thorough tracing of the fortunes of a family." (from Thomas Mann *by Henry Hatfield, 1962)*

Thomas Mann was born in Lübeck. He was the son of a wealthy father, who had been elected twice as the burgomaster of Lübeck. His mother, Bruhn da Silva, came from a German-Portugese-Creole family.

Mann's father died in 1891 and his trading firm was dissolved. The family moved to Munich. Mann was educated at the Lübeck gymnasium and he also spent some time at the University of Munich. Mann then worked with the south German Fire Insurance Company (1894-95). His career as a writer started in the magazine *Simplicissimus*. Mann's first book, DER KLEINE HERR FRIEDMANN, was published in 1898.

During these years Mann became immersed in the writings of the philosophers, Arthur Schopenhauer and Friedrich Nietzsche as well as in the music of composer Richard Wagner. In *Buddenbrooks,* Mann's early masterpiece, he used the technique of the *leitmotif,* which he adapted from Wagner. Mann had started the book in 1897 as a small story about one member of the family. During the writing process the "protracted finger practice with no ulterior advantages" enlarged into a saga of a wealthy Hanseatic family, which declines from strength to decadence. The last Buddenbrook, the young Hanno, becomes a decadent artist.

After publishing Buddenbrooks, Mann concentrated on short novels or novellas. In 1902 he published the novella TONIO KRÖGER, a spiritual autobiography exploring art and discipline. He married in 1905 Katja Pringsheim, the daughter of a wealthy Munich family; they had a total of six children over the ensuing years. KÖNGLICHE HOHEIT (1909) reflected Mann's views on duty and sacrifice. DER TOD IN VENEDIG, 1912, Death in Venice, Mann's famous novel, was inspired by a young, sailor-suited boy, Wladyslaw Moes, whom the author saw in Venice in 1911. Other characters have also their counterparts in real life. However, Tadzio in the book is 14, but Wladyslaw was 11. In the story an author, Gustav von Aschenbach, falls hopelessly in love with a young teenager, Tadzio. Obsessed with the boy, he stays in Venice during a cholera epidemic, and also dies of cholera. The story was adapted into screen by Luchino Visconti, starring Dirk Bogarde and Bjorn Andresen. During World War I Mann supported Kaiser's policy and attacked liberalism. In VON DEUTSCHER REPUBLIK (1923), as a semi-official spokesman for parliamentary democracy, he called the German intellectual to support the new Weimar state.

> *"A man lives not only his personal life, as an individual, but also, consciously or unconsciously, the life of his epoch and his contemporaries." (from* The Magic Mountain, *1924)*

After ten years of work Mann completed his second major work, DER ZAUBERBERG (The Magic Mountain, 1924), a novel about ideas and of lost humanism. It depicted again a fight between liberal and conservative values, enlightened civilized world and nonrational beliefs. Hans Castorp, the protagonist, goes to the elegant tuberculosis sanatorium in Davos to visit his cousin. Castorp is not really ill, but he stays for a period of seven years, and undergoes an advanced education on the Magic Mountain, primarily through speaking and listening. Two men struggle for his soul, Settembrini, an Italian humanist, and Naptha, a radical reactionary, who speaks of blind and irrational faith. Naptha cries out a prophecy that came true in Germany only a decade after publication of the book: "No!" Naphta continued. "The mystery and precept of our age is not liberation and the development of the ego. What our age needs, what it demands, what it will create for itself, is - terror." Naphta challenges Settembrini to a duel with pistols. Settembrini fires into the air, while Naphta kills himself in a rage. Another weird character is Mynheer Peeperkorn who arrives at the Mountain in the company of the beautiful Claudia Chauchat. Castorp falls in love with her at first sight. Claudia returns to Peeperkorn, and Castorp yearns for her deeply. The vitalistic Peeperkorn, who confronts his own impotence, also kills himself. Castorp leaves the sanatorium to join the army at the outbreak of the war. Mann tells the reader that while the young man's chances of survival are not good, the question must be left open.

"I always feel a bit bored when critics assign my own work so definitely and completely to the realm of irony and consider me an ironist through and through, without also taking account of the concept of humor." (Thomas Mann, from Harold Bloom's How to Read and Why, *2000)*

Mann's next major work was the trilogy JOSEPH UND SEINE BRÜDER (1933-42), set in the biblical world. The story about the conflict between personal freedom and political tyranny is based on Genesis 12-50. The first volume recounts the early history of Jacob, and introduces then Joseph, who is the central character. He is sold to Egypt, where he refuses Potiphar's advances and gains his enmity. Joseph develops into a wise man and the savior of his people. During the process of writing the political control in Germany was seized by the Nazis.

> *"He belonged to that cut of present-day lesser artists who don't ask too much of themselves, wish first of all to be happy and amiable, utilize their comfortably small talent to enhance their personal appeal, and play the naïve genius in society. Intentionally childlike, unscrupulous, beyond morality, enjoying everything, and contented with themselves as they are, they are healthy enough to enjoy their little illnesses; and their vanity is in reality quite delightful so long as it is not wounded. But woe to these lesser mimes and their amusements, if they meet with some serious misfortune, some sorrow that can't be toyed with and in which they can find no self-contentment! They will fail at being properly miserable; they will not know how to approach their sorrow; they will go all to pieces . . ." (from 'Loulou', 1921)*

On Hitler's accession Mann moved to Switzerland, where he edited the literary journal *Mass und Wert*, and settled finally in the United States in 1936, where he worked among others at the University of Princeton. LOTTE IN WEIMAR (1939) returned to the world of Goethe's novel *The Sorrows of Young Werther* (1774). In 1941 he moved to Santa Monica, California. Mann lived in the U.S. for ten years, but was disappointed with the American persecution of Communist sympathizers.

Mann admired greatly Russian literature and wrote several essays on Leo Tolstoy and his "undying realism". Especially he loved Tolstoy's *Anna Karenina*. However, he disliked the later Tolstoy and considered him less noble than Goethe. In the essay 'Dostoevsky - With Moderation' (1945) he deals with the author's supposed confession to Turgenev that he had violated an underaged girl. René Wellek has dismissed Mann's speculations and considers the whole business of Dostoevsky's criminality to be totally misconceived (*A History of Modern Criticism*, vol. 7, 1991).

Mann's last great work was DOKTOR FAUSTUS (1947), the story of a composer Adrian Lewerkühn and the progressive destruction of German culture in the two World Wars. In the background of the story was the innovative 12-tone music of Arnold Schönberg. Mann's account of the genesis of *Doctor Faustus* appeared in 1949. In 1947 Mann returned to Europe. Demonstratively he avoided Germany and lived mostly in Switzerland, near Zürich, where he died on August 12, 1955. Mann's parodic and light-hearted novel *Confessions of Felix Krull* was left unfinished.

Rabindranath Tagore

Rabindranath Tagore is the greatest writer in modern Indian literature, Bengali poet, novelist, educator, and an early advocate of Independence for India. Tagore won the Nobel Prize for Literature in 1913. Two years later he was awarded the knighthood, but he surrendered it in 1919 as a protest against the Massacre of Amritsar, where British troops killed some 400 Indian demonstrators. Tagore's influence over Gandhi and the founders of modern India was enormous, but his reputation in the West as a mystic has perhaps mislead his Western readers to ignore his role as a reformer and critic of colonialism.

> *"When one knows thee, then alien there is none, then no door is shut. Oh, grant me my prayer that I may never lose touch of the one in the play of the many." (from* Gitanjali*)*

Rabindranath Tagore was born in Calcutta into a wealthy and prominent Brahman family. His father was Maharishi Debendranath Tagore, a religious reformer and scholar. His mother, Sarada Devi, died when Tagore was very young. He realized that she will never come back when her body was carried through a gate to a place where it was burned. Tagore's grandfather had established a huge financial empire for himself. He helped a number of public projects, such as Calcutta Medical College.

The Tagores tried to combine traditional Indian culture with Western ideas; all the children contributed significantly to Bengali literature and culture. However, in *My Reminiscences* Tagore mentions that it was not until the age of ten when he started to use socks and shoes. And servants beat the children regularly. Tagore, the youngest, started to compose poems at the age of eight. Tagore's first book, a collection of poems, appeared when he was 17; it was published by Tagore's friend who wanted to surprise him.

Tagore received his early education first from tutors and then at a variety of schools. Among them were Bengal Academy where he studied history and culture. At University College, London, he studied law but left after a year as he did not like the weather. Once he gave a beggar a gold coin. It was more than the beggar had expected and he returned it. In England Tagore started to compose the poem 'Bhagna Hridaj' (a broken heart).

In 1883 Tagore married Mrinalini Devi Raichaudhuri, with whom he had two sons and three daughters. In 1890 Tagore moved to East Bengal (now Bangladesh), where he collected local legends and folklore. Between 1893 and 1900 he wrote seven volumes of poetry, including SONAR TARI (The Golden Boat), 1894, and KHANIKA, 1900. This was a highly productive period in Tagore's life, and earned him the rather misleading epitaph 'The Bengali Shelley.' More important was that Tagore wrote in the common language of the people. This was something hard to be accepted among his critics and scholars.

Tagore was the first Indian to bring an element of psychological realism to his novels. Among his early major prose works are CHOCHER BALI (1903, Eyesore) and NASHTANIR (1901, The Broken Nest), which were published first serially. Between 1891 and 1895 he published forty-four short stories in the Bengali periodical, most of them in the monthly journal *Sadhana*.

Deeply Tagore's short stories influenced Indian Literature. 'Punishment', a much anthologized work, was set in a rural village. It describes the oppression of women through the tragedy of the low-caste Rui family. Chandara is a proud, beautiful woman, "buxom, well-rounded, compact and sturdy," her husband, Chidam, is a farm-laborer, who works in the fields with his brother Dukhiram. One day when they return home after whole day of toil and humiliation, Dukhiram kills in anger his sloppy and slovenly wife because his food was not ready. To help his brother, Chidam tells the police that his wife struck her sister-in-law with the farm-knife. Chandara takes the blame on to herself. 'In her thoughts, Chandara was saying to her husband, "I shall give my youth to the gallows instead of you. My final ties in this life will be with them."' Afterwards both Chidam and Dukhiram try to confess that they were guilty but Chandara is convicted. Just before the hanging, the doctor says that her husband wants to see her. "To hell with him," says Chandara.

In 1901 Tagore founded a school outside Calcutta, Visva-Bharati, which was dedicated to the emerging Western and Indian philosophy and education. It become a university in 1921. He produced poems, novels, stories, a history of India, textbooks, and treatises on pedagogy. Tagore's wife died in 1902, and the following year one of his daughters died, and in 1907 Tagore lost his younger son.

Tagore's reputation as a writer was established in the United States and in England after the publication of GITANJALI: SONG OF OFFERINGS, about divinity and human love. The poems were translated into English by the author himself. In the introduction from 1912 William Butler Yates wrote: "These lyrics - which are in the original, my Indians tell me, are full of subtlety of rhythm, of untranslatable delicacies of colour, of metrical invention - which display in their thought a world I have dreamed of all my life long." Tagore's poems were also praised by Ezra Pound, and drew the attention of the Nobel Prize committee. "There is in him the stillness of nature. The poems do not seem to have been produced by storm or by ignition, but seem to show the normal habit of his mind. He is at one with nature, and finds no contradictions. And this is in sharp contrast with the Western mode, where man must be shown attempting to master nature if we are to have "great drama." (Ezra Pound in *Fortnightly Review*, 1 March 1913) However, Tagore also experimented with poetic forms and these works have lost much in translations into other languages.

Much of Tagore's ideology come from the teaching of the Upanishads and from his own beliefs that God can be found through personal purity and service to others. He stressed the need for new world order based on transnational values and ideas, the "unity consciousness." "The soil, in return for her service, keeps the tree tied to her; the sky asks nothing and leaves it free." Politically active in India, Tagore was a supporter of Gandhi, but warned of the dangers of nationalistic thought. Unable to gain ideological support to his views, he retired into relative solitude. Between the years 1916 and 1934 he travelled widely. From his journey to Japan in 1916 he produced articles and books. In 1927, he toured in south-east Asia. *Letters from Java*, which first was serialized in *Vichitra*, was issued as a book, JATRI, in 1929. His Majesty, Riza Shah Pahlavi, invited Tagore to Iran in 1932. On his journeys and lecture tours, Tagore attempted to spread the ideal of uniting East and West. While in Japan he wrote: "The Japanese do not waste their energy in useless screaming and quarreling, and because there is no waste of energy it is not found wanting when required. This calmness and fortitude of body and mind is part of their national self-realization."

Tagore wrote his most important works in Bengali, but he often translated his poems into English. At the age of 70 Tagore took up painting. He was also a composer, setting hundreds of poems to music. Many of his poems are actually songs, and inseparable from their music. Tagore's 'Our Golden Bengal' became the national anthem of Bangladesh. Only hours before he died on August 7, in 1941, Tagore dictated his last poem. His written production, is still not completely collected, and it fills nearly 30 substantial volumes. Tagore remained a well-known and popular author in the West until the end of the 1920s, but nowadays he is not so much read.

V. S. Naipaul

Vidiadhar Surajprasad Naipaul is generally considered the leading novelist of the English-speaking Caribbean, winner of the Nobel Prize in literature 2001. Naipaul's writings dealt with the cultural confusion of the Third World and the problem of an outsider, a feature of his own experience as an Indian in the West Indies, a West Indian in England, and a nomadic intellectual in a postcolonial world. Naipaul has also arisen much controversy because of his politically incorrect views of the "half-made societies." He has constantly refused to avoid unwelcoming topics, characterizing his role as a writer "to look and to look again, to re-look and rethink."

"The facts about Columbus have always been known. In his own writings and in all his actions his egoism is like an exposed deformity; he condemns himself. But the heroic gloss, which is not even his own, has come down through the centuries." (from 'Columbus and Crusoe', in The Overcrowded Barracoon, *1972)*

Vidiadhar Surajprasad Naipaul was born in a small town in Trinidad into a family of Indian Brahmin origin. His father, Seepersad Naipaul, was a correspondent for the Trinidad Guardian. He also published short stories. When Naipaul was six, the family moved to Port of Spain, the capital. Seepersad Naipaul died of a heart attack in 1953 without witnessing the success of his son as a writer. He had encouraged Naipaul in his writing aspirations, telling him in a letter: "Don't be scared of being an artist. D.H. Lawrence was an artist through and through; and, for the time being at any rate, you should think as Lawrence. Remember what he used to say, 'Art for my sake.'"

At the age of 18 he had written his first novel which was rejected by the publisher.

Naipaul was educated at Queen's Royal College, Port of Spain, and in 1950 he won a scholarship to Oxford. In 1949, after having some pictures of himself taken for his application to the university, Naipaul wrote to his elder sister: "I never knew my face was fat. The picture said so. I looked at the Asiatic on the paper and thought that an Indian from India could look no more Indian than I did... I had hoped to send up a striking intellectual pose to the University people, but look what they have got." After a nervous breakdown he tried to commit suicide, but luckily the gas meter ran out. While at Oxford he met Patricia Hale; they married in 1955. She died in 1966 and Naipaul married Nadira Alvi, a divorced Pakistani journalist. On graduation, Naipaul started his career as a freelance writer. During this period Naipaul felt himself rootless, but found his voice as a writer in the mid-1950s, when he started to examine his own Trinidadian background. From 1954 to 1956 Naipaul was a broadcaster for the BBC's Caribbean Voices, and between the years 1957 and 1961 he was a regular fiction reviewer for the *New Statesman*.

Naipaul published his first books in the late 1950s, but they did not make much money for him or his publisher, André Deutsch Limited. However, he knew his value as a writer and refused to write a review for *The Times Literary Supplement* for their usual fee. MIGUEL STREET (1959) was a farewell to Port of Spain, Trinidad. The colorful characters of the sketches include Bogart, who got his name from the film Casablanca, B. Wordsworth who sells his poetry for four cents, and Man-man who in a real mystery to the people of Miguel Street. The narrator is a boy who grows up, starts to earn his own money and finally goes abroad to study. "I left them all and walked briskly towards the aeroplane, not looking back, looking only at my shadow before me, a dancing dwarf on the tarmac." In later works Naipaul gave up comedic tones but in 1960 Charles Poore wrote in his review of the book: "A comparison with "Porgy and Bess" has been suggested. The parallel has at least the merit of reminding us that the whole world is one. In that hospitable mood we might also remember Mark Twain's Tales of Life on the Mississippi. But Miguel Street, in Trinidad, is not really very much like Catfish Row, nor are reminders of nineteenth-century Missouri prevalent. What is true and, if you will, significant about Mr. Naipaul's book is that it presents a world of its own excellently." (*The New York Times*, May 5, 1960)

In 1961 appeared A HOUSE FOR MR BISWAS, often regarded as his masterpiece, which tells the tragicomic story of the search for independence and identity of a Brahmin Indian living in Trinidad. The protagonist, Mohun Biswas, was partly modelled after the author's father. Naipaul has said about this character and his father: "My father was a profounder man in every way. And his wounds are deeper than the other man can say. It's based on him, but it couldn't be the real man." Biswas has been unlucky from his birth, but all he wants is a house of his own - it is the solid basis of his existence. The story, which fuses social comedy and pathos, follows his struggle in variety of jobs, from sign painter to journalist, to his final triumph. Later Naipaul returned to his father in BETWEEN FATHER AND SON (1999), a record of their correspondence in the early 1950s.

In 1961 Naipaul received a grant from the Trinidad government to travel to the Caribbean. His first non-fiction book was THE MIDDLE PASSAGE (1962), in which he described his first revisiting of the West Indies. Its examination of racial tensions made black West Indians call Naipaul a 'racist.' From the wide period of travels in the 1960s and early 1970s in India, South-America, Africa, Iran, Pakistan, Malaysia and the USA, Naipaul produced among others INDIA: A WOUNDED CIVILIZATION (1977), and A BEND IN THE RIVER (1979), a pessimistic novel about Africa, proclaiming the corruptibility of mankind. The story is set in a country very like Zaïre or Uganda. Salim, the narrator is a Muslim, whose family, are Indian traders, who have lived in Africa hundreds of years. Salim sets up a shop in a town on the bend of the river and gains success, which has no future in a country ruled by the Big Man, who is president for life. Again Naipaul's protagonist is an outsider, who realizes that his way of life is almost at its end and eventually he must give up everything. "The bush runs itself. But there is no place to go," says Salim's friend Ferdinand, when he rescues Salim from jail. "The bush" is Naipaul's metaphor for the country and the whole third world. "Africa has no culture," Naipaul has said. Derek Walcott, the West Indian poet who won the Nobel prize for literature in 1992, noted: "If Naipaul's attitude toward Negroes, with its nasty little sneers... was turned on Jews, for example, how many people would praise him for his frankness?"

Since 1950 Naipaul has lived in Britain, but travelled extensively. His essays and travel writings are often negative, unsentimental explorations of West Indian society as in THE MIDDLE PASSAGE (1962). "The steel band used to be regarded as a high manifestation of West Indian culture, but it was a sound I detested." AMONG THE BELIEVERS: AN ISLAMIC JOURNEY (1981) was accused by Muslim readers of narrow and selective vision of Islam. Naipaul searches the sources of the new Islam – and the ideological rage. "Islam sanctified rage – rage about the faith and political rage: one could be like the other. And more than once on this journey I had met sensitive men who were ready to contemplate great convulsions." (from *Among the Believers*) Naipaul's latest travel books include BEYOND BELIEF: ISLAMIC EXCURSIONS AMONG THE CONVERTED PEOPLES (1998), intimate portraits from his journeys to the non-Arab Islamic countries of Indonesia, Iran, Pakistan, and Malaysia. Naipaul tries to understand the fundamentalist fervour that have marked the Western image of the region. "There probably has been no imperialism like that of Islam and the Arabs," he writes. In Iran he meets war veterans, who express their disillusionment and their sense of being manipulated by the mullahs. In Indonesia he meets his former friend, who opposed the Suharto regime, and later became an established figure, an advocate of an Islamicist future. On his first visit to India since he was awarded the Nobel Prize, Naipaul said: "We are not here to celebrate the antiquity of literature in India, but to celebrate modern writing."

In his semi-autobiographical novel THE ENIGMA OF ARRIVAL (1987) Naipaul depicts a writer of Caribbean origin, who finds joys of homecoming in England after wandering years - during which the world stopped being a colony for him. Central themes in Naipaul's works are damaging effects of colonialism upon the people of the Third World, but he doesn't believe in the imported ideas of revolutionaries or the ability of the former colonies to avoid mistakes made by the Western consumer societies. As a writer, he has been compared to Joseph Conrad because of similar pessimistic portrayal of human nature and the themes of exile and alienation. "Barbarism in India is very powerful because it has a religious side," he once stated. In the essay 'Conrad's Darkness' (pub. in THE RETURN OF EVA PERON, 1980) Naipaul sees his own background as "one of the Conradian dark places of the earth."

In the 1990s Naipaul concentrated on non-fiction. In 1994 appeared his long-awaited novel, A WAY IN THE WORLD, an autobiography and a fictional history of colonialism, presenting stories from the times of Sir Walter Raleigh to the nineteenth-century revolutionary Franciso Miranda. In HALF A LIFE (2001), the protagonist is Willie Somerset Chandrasekharan, born in India in the 1930s. He got his second name from the English writer Somerset Maugham, who has met his father. Willie moves to London, drifts in bohemian circles, publishes a book, marries Ana, a woman of mixed African descent, and moves with her to Africa, to her family estate. Willie has problems to come to terms with himself, as the son of a Brahman, who has married an "untouchable." His father is a rebel who ends at a monastery. Willie rebels against his own background and the wishes of his father, with whom he has more in common than he admits. In his wife's home country, in which colonial system is breaking down, Willie is also an outsider. After eighteen years he decides to leave her, and find his true identity. He has lived half a life, a shadow life, but Naipaul doesn't tell what happen's to him. Willie's existential search continues and the rest of his story is left open.

Willie's decision parallels with the history of the relationship between the American writer Paul Theroux and Naipaul. Theroux depicted his decaded long friendship with Naipaul in *Sir Vidia's Shadow* (1998). In this angry and unforgiving book, Theroux eventually is rejected by Naipaul and he realizes he has come out Naipaul's shadow and that he is free. Theroux considered earlier the older writer as his mentor but the friendship ended in a breakup, which Theroux sealed with his bitter accusations. "I had admired his talent. After a while I admired nothing else. Finally I began to wonder about his talent, seriously wondered and doubted it when I found myself skipping pages in his more recent books. In the past I would have said the fault was mine. Now I knew that he could be the monomaniac in print that he was in person." (from *Sir Vidia's Shadow*) - Among Naipaul's several literary awards is the Booker Prize for IN A FREE STATE (1971). He was knighted in 1989 and in 1993 he won the first David Cohen British Literature Prize for "lifetime achievement by a living British writer". Naipaul's manuscripts and extensive archives have been deposited in the University of Tulsa.

Marie Curie

Marie Curie was the first woman to win a Nobel Prize. She was renowned for her work with radioactivity, and it was that work that eventually ended her life.

Maria Sklodowska was born in Warsaw, Poland on November 7, 1867. She was the fifth and the last child of a piano player and teacher Bronsilawa Boguska and mathematics and physics professor, Wladyslaw Sklodowski. Her childhood nickname was Manya. Her father was a freethinker and her mother was a Catholic.

Her family valued education, and so she began her education early. She possessed a remarkable memory. She graduated from secondary school when she was sixteen, receiving a gold medal for her work. Unfortunately her father made some bad investments and she had to go to work at a young age as a teacher, postponing the continuance of her own education. At the age of 18 she became a governess, and put her sister, Bronia, through school with the agreement that Bronia would return the favor and she did.

In 1891 at the age of 24, Sklodowska went to Paris to study mathematics, physics and chemistry at Sorbonne. She studied fervently, and subsisted almost entirely on bread, butter and tea. During her years there she changed the spelling of her name to the French version, Marie.

She met Pierre Curie in Paris while she studied there, and they soon married in a Civil ceremony. Marie had left the Catholic church when she was 20 and Pierre was not a member of any religion, either.

Marie and Pierre Curie devoted themselves to the study of radioactivity, and were among the first to work with radium and polonium. It was Marie Curie who coined the term radioactivity, and she named Polonium after her home country of Poland. Pierre was chiefly concerned with the physical properties of radium and polonium, while Marie worked to isolate radium in its pure state. She and one of Pierre's students, Mr. Debierne, accomplished this, and Marie received her doctorate in 1903 based on her findings. Also in 1903, the Curies won the Nobel Prize for their work along with French physicist, Antoine Henri Bacquerel, who had first discovered natural radioactivity.

Marie and Pierre Curie had two daughters. Irene was born in 1897 and Eve was born in 1904. During their childhood Marie was a physics instructor at the Normal Superior School for girls in Svres, France. In 1904 she became Chief Assistant in Pierre's laboratory.

In 1906, Pierre Curie, whose health had begun to fail due to the work with radioactivity, was hit by a car and killed. This was a deep tragedy for the family, but it strengthened Marie's resolve to continue their work. On May 13, she was appointed to fill Pierre's position and became the first female professor at the Sorbonne.

In 1911 Marie Curie won the Nobel Prize for her achievement of isolating radium and examining its chemical properties. She was the first person ever to receive two Nobel Prizes. In 1914 she co-founded the Radium Institute in Paris and was its first Director. During the First World War, Curie and her daughter, Irene, taught a team of 150 nurses to use X-rays so that bullets could be located in injured soldiers. In 1921 she traveled to the United States where President Warren Harding presented her with a gram of radium purchased with a collection taken up among American Women. In 1922, as a member of the French Academy of Medicine she devoted her work to medical applications of radioactive substances. In 1932, the Radium Institute of Warsaw, Poland was opened under the directorship of Marie's sister, Bronia.

Marie Curie died at the age of 67 in 1934 of leukemia, brought on by her years of exposure to high levels of radiation. Her cremated remains are kept in the Pantheon in Paris. She was the first woman to be honored in this way for her personal achievements. After her death the Radium Institute was renamed as The Curie Institute.

In 1935, Curie's daughter, Irene Joliot-Curie won a Nobel Prize for Chemistry making them the first mother and daughter to share this honour.

Kofi Annan

Kofi Annan of Ghana is the seventh Secretary-General of the United Nations. The first Secretary-General to be elected from the ranks of United Nations staff, he began his first term on 1 January 1997. On 29 June 2001, acting on a recommendation by the Security Council, the General Assembly appointed him by acclamation to a second term of office, beginning on 1 January 2002 and ending on 31 December 2006.

Mr. Annan's priorities as Secretary-General have been to revitalize the United Nations through a comprehensive programme of reform; to strengthen the Organization's traditional work in the areas of development and the maintenance of international peace and security; to encourage and advocate human rights, the rule of law and the universal values of equality, tolerance and human dignity found in the United Nations Charter; and to restore public confidence in the Organization by reaching out to new partners and, in his words, by "bringing the United Nations closer to people".

Mr. Annan was born in Kumasi, Ghana, on 8 April 1938. He studied at the University of Science and Technology in Kumasi and completed his undergraduate work in Economics at Macalester College in St. Paul, Minnesota, U.S.A., in 1961. From 1961 to 1962, he undertook graduate studies in Economics at the Institut universitaire des hautes études internationales in Geneva. As a 1971-1972 Sloan Fellow at the Massachusetts Institute of Technology, Mr. Annan received a Master of Science degree in Management.

Mr. Annan joined the United Nations System in 1962 as an administrative and budget officer with the World Health

Organization (WHO) in Geneva. Since then, he has served with the UN Economic Commission for Africa (ECA) in Addis Ababa; the United Nations Emergency Force (UNEF II) in Ismailia; the Office of the United Nations High Commissioner for Refugees (UNHCR) in Geneva; and, at UN Headquarters in New York, as Assistant Secretary-General for Human Resources Management and Security Coordinator for the UN System (1987-1990) and Assistant Secretary-General for Programme Planning, Budget and Finance, and Controller (1990-1992).

In 1990, following the invasion of Kuwait by Iraq, Mr. Annan was asked by the Secretary-General, as a special assignment, to facilitate the repatriation of more than 900 international staff and citizens of Western countries from Iraq. He subsequently led the first United Nations team negotiating with Iraq on the sale of oil to fund purchases of humanitarian aid.

Before being appointed Secretary-General, Mr. Annan served as Assistant Secretary-General for Peace-keeping Operations (March 1992-February 1993) and then as Under-Secretary-General (March 1993-December 1996). His tenure as Under-Secretary-General coincided with unprecedented growth in the size and scope of United Nations peacekeeping operations, with a total deployment, at its peak in 1995, of almost 70,000 military and civilian personnel from 77 countries. From November 1995 to March 1996, following the Dayton Peace Agreement that ended the war in Bosnia and Herzegovina, Mr. Annan served as Special Representative of the Secretary-General to the former Yugoslavia, overseeing the transition in Bosnia and Herzegovina from the United Nations Protection Force (UNPROFOR) to the multinational Implementation Force (IFOR) led by the North Atlantic Treaty Organization (NATO).

As Secretary-General, Mr. Annan's first major initiative was his plan to reform, "Renewing the United Nations", which was presented to the Member States in July 1997 and has been pursued ever since with an emphasis on improving coherence and coordination. His April 1998 report to the Security Council on "The Causes of Conflict and the Promotion of Durable Peace and Sustainable Development in Africa" was among several efforts to maintain the international community's commitment to Africa, the most disadvantaged of the world's regions.

He has used his good offices in several delicate political situations. These included an attempt in 1998 to gain Iraq's compliance with Security Council resolutions; a mission in 1998 to help promote the transition to civilian rule in Nigeria; an agreement in 1999 to resolve a stalemate between Libya and the Security Council over the 1988 Lockerbie bombing; diplomacy in 1999 to forge an international response to violence in East Timor; the certification of Israel's withdrawal from Lebanon in September 2000, and further efforts, since the renewed outbreak of violence in September 2000, to encourage Israelis and Palestinians to resolve their differences through peaceful negotiations based on Security Council resolutions 242 and 338 and the principle of "land for peace".

Mr. Annan has also sought to improve the status of women in the Secretariat and to build closer partnerships with civil society, the private sector and other non-State sectors whose strengths complement those of the United Nations. In particular, he has called for a "Global Compact" involving leaders of the world business community as well as labour and civil society organizations, aimed at enabling all the world's people to share the benefits of globalization and embedding the global market in values and practices that are fundamental to meeting socio-economic needs.

In April 2000, he issued a Millennium Report, entitled "We the Peoples: The Role of the United Nations in the 21st Century", calling on Member States to commit themselves to an action plan for ending poverty and inequality, improving education, reducing HIV/AIDS, safeguarding the environment and protecting people from deadly conflict and violence. The Report formed the basis of the Millennium Declaration adopted by Heads of State and Government at the Millennium Summit, held at UN Headquarters in September 2000.

In April 2001, the Secretary-General issued a five-point "Call to Action" to address the HIV/AIDS epidemic — which he described as his "personal priority". And he proposed the establishment of Global AIDS and Health Fund to serve as a mechanism for some of the increased spending needed to help developing countries confront the crisis.

On 10 December 2001, the Secretary-General and the United Nations received the Nobel Peace Prize. In conferring the Prize, the Nobel Committee said Mr. Annan "had been pre-eminent in bringing new life to the Organization". In also conferring the Prize on the world body, the Committee said that it wished "to proclaim that the only negotiable road to global peace and cooperation goes by way of the United Nations".

The Secretary-General is fluent in English, French and several African languages. He is married to Nane Annan, of Sweden, a lawyer and artist who has great interest in understanding the work of the United Nations. Two issues of particular concern to her are HIV/AIDS and education for women. She has also written a book for children about the United Nations. Mr. and Mrs. Annan have three children.

Yasser Arafat

 ohammed Abdel-Raouf Arafat As Qudwa al-Hussaeini was born on 24 August 1929 in Cairo. His father a textile merchant was a Palestinian with some Egyptian ancestry and his mother belonged to an old Palestinian family in Jerusalem. She died when Yasser, as he was called, was five years old, and he was sent to live with his maternal uncle in Jerusalem, the capital of Palestine, then under British rule, which the Palestinians were opposing. He has revealed little about his childhood, but one of his earliest memories is of British soldiers breaking into his uncle's house after midnight, beating members of the family and smashing furniture.

After four years in Jerusalem, his father brought him back to Cairo, where an older sister took care of him and his siblings. Arafat never mentions his father, who was not close to his children. Arafat did not attend his father's funeral in 1952.

In Cairo, before he was seventeen Arafat was smuggling arms to Palestine which used to be against the British and the Jews. At nineteen, during the war between the Jews and the Arab states, Arafat left his studies at the University of Faud (later Cairo University) to fight against the Jews in the Gaza area. The defeat of the Arabs and the establishment of the state of Israel left him in such despair that he applied for a visa to study at the University of Texas. Recovering his spirits and retaining his dream of an independent Palestinian homeland, he returned to Faud University to major in engineering but spent most of his time as leader of the Palestinian students.

He did manage to get his degree in 1956, worked briefly in Egypt and then resettled in Kuwait. He was employed in the department of public works and successfully ran his own contracting firm. He spent all his spare time in political activities, to which he contributed most of the profits. In 1958 he and his friends founded Al-Fatah, an underground network of secret cells, which in 1959 began to publish a magazine advocating armed struggle against Israel. At the end of 1964 Arafat left Kuwait to become a full-time revolutionary, organising Fatah raids into Israel from Jordan.

It was also in 1964 that the Palestine Liberation Organisation (PLO) was established, under the sponsorship of the Arab League, bringing together a number of groups all working to free Palestine for the Palestinians. The Arab states favoured a more conciliatory policy than Fatah's, but after their defeat by Israel in the 1967 Six-Day War, Fatah emerged from the underground as the most powerful and best organised of the groups making up the PLO. It took over the organisation in 1969 when Arafat became the Chairman of the PLO Executive committee. The PLO was no longer to be something of a puppet organisation of the Arab states, wanting to keep the Palestinians quiet, but an independent nationalist organisation, based in Jordan.

Arafat developed the PLO into a state within the state of Jordan with its own military forces. King Hussein of Jordan, disturbed by its guerrilla attacks on Israel and other violent methods, eventually expelled the PLO from his country. Arafat sought to build a similar organisation in Lebanon, but this time was driven out by an Israeli military invasion. He kept the organization alive, however, by moving its headquarters to Tunis. He was a survivor himself, escaping death in an airplane crash, surviving any assassination attempts by Israeli intelligence agencies, and recovering from a serious stroke.

His life was one of constant travel, moving from country to country to promote the Palestinian cause, always keeping his movements secret, as he did any details about his private life. Even his marriage to Suha Tawil, a Palestinian half his age, was kept secret for some fifteen months. She had already begun significant humanitarian activities at home, especially for disabled children, but the prominent part she took in the public events in Oslo was a surprise for many Arafat-watchers. Since then, their daughter, Zahwa, named after Arafat's mother, has been born.

The period after the expulsion from Lebanon was a low time for Arafat and the PLO. Then the *intifada* (shaking) protest movement strengthened Arafat by directing world attention to the difficult plight of the Palestinians. In 1988 came a change of policy. In a speech at a special United Nations session held in Geneva, Switzerland, Arafat declared that the PLO renounced terrorism and supported "the right of all parties concerned in the Middle East conflict, to live in peace and security, including the state of Palestine, Israel and other neighbours".

The prospects for a peace agreement with Israel now brightened. After a setback when the PLO supported Iraq in the Persian Gulf War of 1991, the peace process began in earnest, leading to the Oslo Accords of 1993.

This agreement included provision for the Palestinian elections which took place in early 1996, and Arafat was elected President of the Palestine Authority. Like other Arab regimes in the area, however, Arafat's governing style tended to be more dictatorial than democratic. When the right-wing government of Benjamin Netanyahu came to power in Israel in 1996, the peace process slowed down considerably. Much depends upon the nature of the new Israeli government, which will result from the elections to be held in 1999.

Dalai Lama

His Holiness the XIVth, Dalai Lama, Tenzin Gyatso, is the spiritual and temporal leader of the Tibetan people. He was born in a small village called Takster in northeastern Tibet. Born to a peasant family, His Holiness was recognized at the age of two, in accordance with Tibetan tradition, as the reincarnation of his predecessor, the 13th Dalai Lama. The Dalai Lamas are the manifestations of the Bodhisattva of Compassion, who chose to reincarnate to serve the people. Dalai Lama means Ocean of Wisdom. Tibetans normally refer to His Holiness as *Yeshin Norbu*, the Wish-fulfilling Gem, or simply, *Kundun*, meaning The Presence.

Education in Tibet

He began his education at the age of six and completed the Geshe Lharampa Degree (Doctorate of Buddhist Philosophy) when he was 25. At 24, he took the preliminary examination at each of the three monastic universities: Drepung, Sera and Ganden. The final examination was held in the Jokhang, Lhasa, during the annual Monlam Festival of Prayer, held in the first month of every year. In the morning he was examined by 30 scholars on logic. In the afternoon, he debated with 15 scholars on the subject of the Middle Path, and in the evening, 35 scholars tested his knowledge of the canon of monastic discipline and the study of metaphysics. His Holiness passed the examinations with honours, conducted before a vast audience of monk scholars.

Leadership Responsibilities

In 1950, at 16, His Holiness was called upon to assume full political power as Head of State and Government when Tibet was threatened by the might of China. In 1954 he went to Peking to talk with Mao Tse-Tung and other Chinese leaders, including Chou En-Lai and Deng Xiaoping. In 1956, while visiting India to attend the 2500th Buddha Jayanti, he had a series of meetings with Prime Minister Nehru and Premier Chou about deteriorating conditions in Tibet. In 1959 he was forced into exile in India after the Chinese military occupation of Tibet. Since 1960 he has resided in Dharamsala, aptly known as "Little Lhasa", the seat of the Tibetan Government-in-Exile.

In the early years of exile, His Holiness appealed to the United Nations on the question of Tibet, resulting in three resolutions adopted by the General Assembly in 1959, 1961 and 1965. In 1963, His Holiness promulgated a draft constitution for Tibet which assures a democratic form of government. In the last two decades, His Holiness has set up educational, cultural and religious institutions which have made major contributions towards the preservation of the Tibetan identity and its rich heritage. He has given many teachings and initiations, including the rare Kalachakra Initiation, which he has conducted more than any of his predecessors.

His Holiness continues to present new initiatives to resolve the Tibetan issues. At the Congressional Human Rights Caucus in 1987 he proposed a Five-Point Peace Plan as a first step towards resolving the future status of Tibet. This plan calls for the designation of Tibet as a zone of peace, an end to the massive transfer of ethnic Chinese into Tibet, restoration of fundamental human rights and democratic freedoms and the abandonment of China's use of Tibet for nuclear weapon production and the dumping of nuclear waste, as well as urging "earnest negotiations" on the future of Tibet and relations between the Tibetan and Chinese people. In Strasbourg, France, on June 15, 1988, he elaborated on this Five-Point Peace Plan and proposed the creation of a self-governing democratic Tibet, "in association with the People's Republic of China." In his address,

Dalai Lama said that this represented "the most realistic means by which to re-establish Tibet's separate identity and restore the fundamental rights of the Tibetan people while accommodating China's own interests." His Holiness emphasized that "whatever the outcome of the negotiations with the Chinese may be, the Tibetan people themselves must be the ultimate deciding authority."

Contact with the West

Unlike his predecessors, His Holiness has met and talked with many Westerners and has visited the United States, Canada, Western Europe, the United Kingdom, the Soviet Union, Mongolia, Greece, Japan, Thailand, Malaysia, Singapore, Indonesia, Nepal, Costa Rica, Mexico, the Vatican, China and Australia. He has met religious leaders from all these countries.

His Holiness met the late Pope Paul VI at the Vatican in 1973, and His Holiness Pope John Paul II in 1980, 1982, 1986 and 1988. At a press conference in Rome, His Holiness Dalai Lama outlined his hopes for the meeting with John Paul II: "*We live in a period of great crisis, a period of troubling world developments. It is not possible to find peace in the soul without security and harmony between the people. For this reason, I look forward with faith and hope to my meeting with the Holy Father; to an exchange of ideas and feelings, and to his suggestions, so as to open the door to a progressive pacification between people.*"

In 1981, His Holiness talked with the Archbishop of Canterbury, Dr Robert Runcie, and with other leaders of the Anglican Church in London. He also met leaders of the Roman Catholic and Jewish communities and spoke at an interfaith service in his honour by the World Congress of Faiths. His talk focused on the commonality of faiths and the need for unity among different religions: "*I always believe that it is much better to have a variety of religions, a variety of philosophies, rather than one single religion or philosophy. This is necessary because of the different mental dispositions of each human being. Each religion has certain unique ideas or techniques, and learning about them can only enrich one's own faith."*

Recognition by the West

Since his first visit to the west in the early 1970s, His Holiness' reputation as a scholar and man of peace has grown steadily. In recent years, a number of western universities and institutions have conferred Peace Awards and honorary Doctorate Degrees upon His Holiness in recognition of his distinguished writings in Buddhist philosophy and of his distinguished leadership in the service of freedom and peace.

Universal Responsibility

During his travels abroad, His Holiness has spoken strongly for better understanding and respect among the different faiths of the world. Towards this end, His Holiness has made numerous appearances in interfaith services, imparting the message of universal responsibility, love, compassion and kindness. *"The need for simple human-to-human relationships is becoming increasingly urgent . . . Today the world is smaller and more interdependent. One nation's problems can no longer be solved by itself completely. Thus, without a sense of universal responsibility, our very survival becomes threatened. Basically, universal responsibility is feeling for other people's suffering just as we feel our own. It is the realization that even our enemy is entirely motivated by the quest for happiness. We must recognize that all beings want the same thing that we want. This is the way to achieve a true understanding, unfettered by artificial consideration."*

Mikhail Gorbachev

Mikhail Sergeevich Gorbachev was born in the village of Privolnoye near Stavropol, Russia in 1931. He also worked on a collective farm, which in 1949 exceeded its harvest plan awarding young Gorbachev his first award, the Order of the Red Banner of Labor. Mikhail Gorbachev became a candidate member of the Communist Party in the following year and a full member in 1952. Also, in 1950, he entered the Moscow State University's Law School and graduated in 1955.

Gorbachev married Raisa Titorenko, a philosophy student from the Moscow State University in 1956 and was appointed the First Secretary of the Stavropol City Komsomol in the same year. Their daughter, Irina, was born later that same year. Gorbachev continued his political climb as the Department Head of Propaganda and the Second Secretary for the Kraicom (District Committee) in Stavropol. In 1961, he became a delegate to the 22nd Party Congress and accepted a position as Party Organizer of one of the 16 territorial-production agricultural units in Stavropol Krai. This marked Gorbachev's departure from Komsomol work and his beginning in mainline Party work. Later that year Gorbachev enrolled himself in The Department of Agricultural Economy at the Stavropol Agricultural Institute on a five-year correspondence course. In December Gorbachev was moved to the position of Head of the Department of Party Organs, Stavropol Kraikom, where he remained until 1966 when he was appointed the First Secretary of the Stavropol Gorkom (City Committee).

In 1967, Gorbachev graduated from Stavropol Agriculture Institute with an agriculture economy degree and was appointed Second Secretary Stavropol Kraikom, responsible for agriculture a year later. His performance continues to warrant his climb and in 1970, he was appointed the First Secretary of the Stavropol Kraikom and soon after was elected full member of the Central Committee at the 24th Party Congress. With this post, he became the Stavropol Area Representative in the Supreme Soviet in 1974. He travelled to West Germany in 1975 as head of an official delegation, on invitation of a local communist party.

Gorbachev's phenomenal success was not all due to his own tenacity but also to the success of Kulakov, his superior throughout Gorbachev's political history in Stavropol. Kulakov showed himself as a very efficient agriculturalist and was appointed Head of Agriculture for the Central Committee in 1964. Kulakov implemented the "Ipatovsky Method" of harvesting in the Stavrapol area with the help of Gorbachev and in 1977, Stavropol overfulfilled it's harvest plan and the "Ipatovsky Method" was declared a complete success. Kulakov and Gorbachev were rocketed into the national limelight as Gorbachev was interviewed on the front page of Pravda, the Communist Party's newspaper. Later that year, Gorbachev received the honor of being appointed to the editorial commission responsible for the final draft of the new Soviet Constitution. In 1978, Gorbachev met Brezhnev and Chernenko to give a report on the good harvest again achieved by the Stavropol region. Gorbachev received the Order of the October Revolution later that year.

By January of 1979, as Secretary of Central Committee in charge of Agriculture following Kulakov's death, Gorbachev was 28th in the Party Hierarchy. In November of that year he became a candidate member of the Politburo. As Head of Agriculture, Gorbachev began work on Brezhnev's 10-year Food Plan in 1980, but several bad harvests left Gorbachev's fate in limbo. Brezhnev's death in 1982 drew attention away from Gorbachev's seeming failures. He then began focusing on other national duties and in 1983, he headed up a Soviet delegation to Canada and later that year, he was left in charge of day-to-day operations while Andropov was on vacation. Gorbachev also headed the

Crisis Management Team in charge of the Korean Air Liner incident in Sakhalin.

Andropov died in February 1984. Gorbachev moved up to second in command behind Chernenko who was elected General Secretary shortly thereafter. Due to Gorbachev's aptitude in foreign affairs, he was appointed chairman of the Supreme Soviet Foreign Affairs Commission. In this position, Gorbachev first meets several top leaders of the world's nations. This post did not last long due to Chernenko's death in 1985. In March, Gorbachev was elected General Secretary of the Central Committee and took control of the Union. Gorbachev was not Chernenko's preferred choice as it was Victor Grishin was. This led to some political turmoil at the beginning of Gorbachev's reign, but as is usually true with Soviet leaders, his opponents were soon removed and replaced with loyal subjects.

In 1989 the Soviet Bloc of states experienced an unprecedented fracturing which featured establishments of democratic politics and the distancing of several states from Soviet Russian control. In 1990 the Russian dominated Union of Soviet Socialist Republics was distressed by the rival policies of Gorbachev, of traditionalists who blamed him for importing destabilising foreign ideas without producing any real benefits, of Boris Yeltsin who held that yet more changes were needed to move Russia towards becoming a democracy, and of diverse (and often competing) nationalisms that hoped to exploit the new political climate in their efforts to secure localised nationalist objectives.In 1990 he was awarded the Nobel Peace Prize for his foreign policy initiatives.

Gorbachev continued to press for democratization in the Soviet Union and permitted free elections in Russia and the other republics of the Soviet Union. He survived an attempted coup by Communist hardliners in 1991 but relinquished office after the elected presidents of the constituent republics and undertook to replace the old Soviet Union with a Confederation of Independent States.

Jimmy Carter

Jimmy Carter (James Earl Carter, Jr.) was thirty-ninth president of the United States. He was born on October 1, 1924, in the small farming town of Plains, Georgia, and grew up in the nearby community of Archery. His father, James Earl Carter, Sr., was a farmer and businessman; his mother, Lillian Gordy, a registered nurse.

He was educated in the Plains Public School. He attended Georgia Southwestern College and the Georgia Institute of Technology, and received a B.S. degree from the United States Naval Academy in 1946. In the Navy he became a submariner, serving in both the Atlantic and Pacific fleets and rising to the rank of lieutenant. Chosen by Admiral Hyman Rickover for the nuclear submarine program, he was assigned to Schenectady, N.Y., where he took graduate work at Union College in reactor technology and nuclear physics, and served as Senior Officer to the pre-commissioning crew of the Seawolf, the second nuclear submarine.

On July 7, 1946, he married Rosalynn Smith of Plains. When his father died in 1953, he resigned his naval commission and returned with his family in Georgia. He took over the Carter farms, and he and Rosalynn operated. The Carter Warehouse in Plains, a general-purpose seed and farm supply company. He quickly became a leader of the community, serving on county boards, supervising education, the hospital authority, and the library. In 1962 he won election to the Georgia Senate. He lost his first gubernatorial campaign in 1966, but won the next election, becoming Georgia's 76th governor on January 12, 1971.

He was the Democratic National Committee campaign Chairman for the 1974 congressional and gubernatorial elections.

On December 12, 1974, he announced his candidacy for President of the United States. He won his party's nomination on the first ballot at the 1976 Democratic National Convention, and was elected president on November 2, 1976.

Jimmy Carter served as president from January 20, 1977 to January 20, 1981. Significant foreign policy accomplishments of his administration included the Panama Canal treaties, the Camp David Accords, the treaty of peace between Egypt and Israel, the SALT II treaty with the Soviet Union, and the establishment of U.S. diplomatic relations with the People's Republic of China. He championed human rights throughout the world. On the domestic side, the administration's achievements included a comprehensive energy program conducted by a new Department of Energy. The plan administered deregulation in energy, transportation, communications and finance; major educational programs under a new Department of Education; and major environmental protection legislation, including the Alaska National Interest Lands Conservation Act.

President Carter is the author of seventeen books, many of which are now in revised editions: *Why Not the Best?* 1975, 1996; *A Government as Good as Its People*, 1977, 1996; *Keeping Faith: Memoirs of a President*, 1982, 1995; *Negotiation: The Alternative to Hostility*, 1984; *The Blood of Abraham*, 1985, 1993; *Everything to Gain: Making the Most of the Rest of Your Life*, written with Rosalynn Carter, 1987, 1995; *An Outdoor Journal*, 1988, 1994; *Turning Point: A Candidate, a State, and a Nation Come of Age*, 1992, *Talking Peace: A Vision for the Next Generation*, 1993, 1995; *Always a Reckoning*, 1995; *The Little Baby Snoogle-Fleejer*, illustrated by Amy Carter, 1995; *Living Faith*, 1996; *Sources of Strength: Meditations on Scripture for a Living Faith*, 1997; *The Virtues of Aging*, 1998; *An Hour before Daylight: Memories of a Rural Boyhood*, 2001; *Christmas in Plains: Memories*, 2001; and *The Nobel Peace Prize Lecture*, 2002. In 2003, he published his first novel, *The Hornet's Nest*, a story of the American Revolution.

In 1982, he became University Distinguished Professor at Emory University in Atlanta, Georgia, and founded The Carter Center. Actively guided by President Carter, the nonpartisan and nonprofit Center addresses national and international issues of public policy. Carter Center fellows, associates, and staff join with President Carter in efforts to resolve conflict, promote democracy, protect human rights, and prevent disease and other afflictions. Through the Global 2000 program, the Center advances in health and agriculture in the developing world.

President Carter and The Carter Center have engaged in conflict mediation in Ethiopia and Eritrea (1989), North Korea (1994), Liberia (1994), Haiti (1994), Bosnia (1994), Sudan (1995), the Great Lakes region of Africa (1995-96), Sudan and Uganda (1999), and Venezuela (2002-2003). Under his leadership The Carter Center has sent forty-five international electionmonitoring delegations to elections in the Americas, Africa, and Asia. These include Panama (1989), Nicaragua (1990), Guyana (1992), Venezuela (1998), Nigeria (1999), Indonesia (1999), East Timor (1999), Mexico (2000), China (2001), and Jamaica (2002).

The permanent facilities of The Carter Presidential Center were dedicated in October 1986 and include the Jimmy Carter Library and Museum, administered by the National Archives. Also open to visitors is the Jimmy Carter National Historic Site in Plains, administered by the National Park Service.

Jimmy and Rosalynn Carter volunteer one week a year for Habitat for Humanity, a nonprofit organization that helps needy people in the United States and in other countries to renovate and build homes for themselves. He also teaches Sunday school and is a deacon in the Maranatha Baptist Church of Plains. For recreation, he enjoys fly-fishing, woodworking, jogging, cycling, tennis, and skiing. The Carters have three sons, a daughter, eight grandsons, and three granddaughters.

Mother Teresa

Mother Teresa was born on August 27, 1910, in Skopje, Macedonia, as Gonxhe Bojaxhiu from Albanian parents Nikollë and Drandafille Bojaxhiu. Her father was a successful and well known contractor, and her mother was a housewife. She was the youngest of three children. Mother Teresa's family was a devoted catholic family, they prayed every evening and went to church almost everyday. It was her family's generosity, care for the poor and the less fortunate that made a great impact on young Mother Teresa's life.

By age 12, she had made up her mind, that her vocation was aiding the poor. She decided to become a nun, travelled to Dublin, Ireland, to join the Sisters of Loretto. After about a year in Ireland, she left to join the Loretto convent in the northeast Indian city of Darjeeling, where she spent 17 years teaching and being Principal of St.Mary's High School in Calcutta.

In 1946, her life changed forever while riding a train to the mountain town of Darjeeling to recover from suspected tuberculosis, on the 10th of September she said she received a calling from God "to serve him among the poorest of the poor." Less than a year later she got permission to leave her order and moved to Calcutta's slums to set up her first school. "Sister Agnes" who was a former student, becomes Mother Teresa's first follower. Others soon followed and papal approval arrives to create a religious order of nuns called the Missionaries of Charity.

The foundation was celebrated on October 7 1950 as the feast of the Holy Rosary. To identify herself with the poor she chose a plain white sari with a blue border and a simple cross pinned to her left shoulder.

Their mission is as she would say when she accepted the Nobel Peace Prize: "to care for the hungry, the naked, the homeless, the crippled, the blind, the lepers, all those people who feel unwanted, unloved, uncared for throughout society, people that have become a burden to the society and are shunned by everyone."

With the help of the Calcutta officials she converted a portion of the abandoned temple of Kali, the Hindu goddess of death and destruction into Kalighat Home for the Dying, where even the poorest people would die with dignity. Soon after she opened Nirmal Hriday ("Pure Heart"), a home for the dying, Shanti Nagar (Town of Peace), a leper colony and later her first orphanage. Mother Teresa and the sisters continued opening houses all over India caring for the poor, washing their wounds, soothing their sores, making them feel wanted. But her order's work spread across the world after 1965, when Pope Paul VI granted Mother Teresa's request to globally expand her order. Whether it was in Ethiopia feeding the hungry, the ghettos of South Africa or whether it was her native country Albania when the communist regime collapsed, Calcutta's Mother Teresa "the living saint" was there. In 1982, at the height of the siege in Beirut she convinced the parties to stop the war so she could rescue 37 sick children trapped inside. Mother Teresa became a symbol of untiring commitment to the poor and suffering.

She was probably the most admired women of all time, received many rewards and prices for her outstanding work and she used her reputation traveling all over the world raising money and support for her causes.

1962: She received the Padhma Shri prize for "extraordinary services".

1971: Pope Paul VI honors Mother Teresa by awarding her the first Pope John XXIII Peace Prize.

1972: Government of India presents her with the Jawaharlal Nehru Award for International Understanding.

1979: Wins Nobel Peace Prize

1985: She suffered a heart attack while in Rome visiting Pope John Paul II.

1989: Another almost fatal heart attack, a pacemaker is implanted.

1985: President Reagan presents her the Medal of Freedom, the highest U.S. Civilian Award.

1996: She becomes only the fourth person in the world to receive an honorary U.S. Citizenship.

When she received the Nobel Prize she wore the same trademark 1$ sari and convinced the committee to cancel a dinner in her honor, using the money instead to " feed 400 poor children for a year in India"

Today Mother Teresa's Missionaries of Charity has 570 missions all over the world, comprising of 4000 nuns, a brotherhood of 300 members and over 100,000 lay volunteers operating homes for AIDS, leprosy and tuberculosis patients; soup kitchens, children's and family counseling programs, orphanages, and schools.

Mother Teresa's health was deteriorating, partly due to her age, part from the conditions where she was living, part from her trips all over the world, opening new houses and raising money for the poor.

1991: She suffered pneumonia in Tijuana, Mexico which led to heart failure.

1996: Suffered malaria, chest infection and undergoes heart surgery.

On march 13th 1997: Sister Nirmala is selected as Mother Teresa's successor.

September 5th 1997 : The world learns that Mother Teresa "Angel Of Mercy" has died at age of 87.

Nelson Mandela

Nelson Mandela's greatest pleasure, his most private moment, is watching the sunset with the music of Handel or Tchaikovsky playing.

Locked up in his cell during daylight hours, deprived of music, both these simple pleasures were denied him for decades. With his fellow prisoners, concerts were organised when possible, particularly at Christmas time, where they would sing. Nelson Mandela finds music very uplifting, and takes a keen interest not only in European classical music but also in African choral music and the many talents in South African music. But one voice stands out above all - that of Paul Robeson, whom he describes as our hero.

The years in jail reinforced habits that were already entrenched: the disciplined eating regime of an athlete began in the 1940s, as did the early morning exercise. Still today Nelson Mandela is up by 4.30am, irrespective of how late he has worked the previous evening. By 5am he begins his exercise routine that lasts at least an hour. Breakfast is by 6.30, when the days newspapers are read the day's work begins.

With a standard working day of at least 12 hours, time management is critical and Nelson Mandela is extremely impatient with unpunctuality, regarding it as insulting to those whom he deals with.

When speaking of the extensive travelling he has undertaken since his release from prison, Nelson Mandela says: "I was helped when preparing for my release by the biography of Pandit Nehru, who wrote of what happens when you leave jail. My daughter Zinzi says that she grew up without a father, who, when he returned, became a father of the nation. This has placed a great responsibility on my shoulders. And wherever I travel, I immediately begin to miss the familiar - the mine dumps, the colour and smell that is uniquely South African, and, above all, the people. I do not like to be away for any length of time. For me, there is no place like home."

Mandela accepted the Nobel Peace Prize as an accolade to all people who have worked for peace and stood against racism. It was as much an award to his person as it was to the ANC and all South Africa's people. In particular, he regards it as a tribute to the people of Norway who stood against apartheid while many in the world were silent.

He says: we know it was Norway that provided resources for farming; thereby enabling us to grow food; resources for education and vocational training and the provision of accommodation over the years in exile. The reward for all this sacrifice will be the attainment of freedom and democracy in South Africa, in an open society which respects the rights of all individuals. That goal is now in sight, and we have to thank the people and governments of Norway and Sweden for the tremendous role they played.

Personal Tastes

- Breakfast of plain porridge, with fresh fruit and fresh milk.

- A favourite is the traditionally prepared meat of a freshly slaughtered sheep, and the delicacy Amarhewu (fermented corn-meal).

Biographical Details

Nelson Rolihlahla Mandela was born in a village near Umtata in the Transkei on the 18 July 1918. His father was the Principal Councillor to the Acting Paramount Chief of Thembuland. After his father's death, the young Rolihlahla became the Paramount Chief's ward to be groomed to assume high office. However, influenced by the cases that came before the Chief's court, he was determined to become a lawyer. Hearing the elders stories of his ancestors valour during the wars of resistance in defence of their fatherland, he dreamed also of making his own contribution to the freedom struggle of his people.

After receiving primary education at a local mission school, Nelson Mandela was sent to Healdtown, Wesleyan Secondary School of some repute where he matriculated. He then enrolled at the University College of Fort Hare for the Bachelor of Arts Degree where he was elected onto the Student's Representative Council. He was suspended from college for joining in a protest boycott. He went to Johannesburg where he completed his BA by correspondence, took articles of clerkship and commenced study for his LLB. He entered politics in earnest while studying in Johannesburg by joining the African National Congress in 1942.

At the height of the Second World War a small group of young Africans, members of the African National Congress, banded together under the leadership of Anton Lembede. Among them were William Nkomo, Walter Sisulu, Oliver R. Tambo, Ashby P. Mda and Nelson Mandela. Starting out with 60 members, all of whom were residing around the Witwatersrand, these young people set themselves the formidable task of transforming the ANC into a mass movement, deriving its strength and motivation from the unlettered millions of working people in the towns and countryside, the peasants in the rural areas and the professionals.

Their chief contention was that the political tactics of the old guard' leadership of the ANC, reared in the tradition of constitutionalism and polite petitioning of the government of the day, were proving inadequate to the tasks of national emancipation. In opposition to the old guard', Lembede and his colleagues espoused a radical African Nationalism grounded in the principle of national self-determination. In September 1944 they came together to found the African National Congress Youth League (ANCYL).

Mandela soon impressed his peers by his disciplined work and consistent effort and was elected to the Secretaryship of the Youth League in 1947. By painstaking work, campaigning at the grassroots and through its mouthpiece Inyaniso' (Truth) the ANCYL was able to canvass support for its policies amongst the ANC membership. At the 1945 annual conference of the ANC, two of the League leaders, Anton Lembede and Ashby Mda, were elected onto the National Executive Committee (NEC). Two years later another Youth League leader, Oliver R. Tambo became a member of the NEC.

Spurred on by the victory of the National Party which won the 1948 all-White elections on the platform of Apartheid, at the 1949 Annual Conference, the Programme of Action, inspired by the Youth League, which advocated the weapons of boycott, strike, civil disobedience and non-co-operation was accepted as official ANC policy.

The Programme of Action had been drawn up by a sub-committee of the ANCYL, composed of David Bopape, Ashby Mda, Nelson Mandela, James Njongwe, Walter Sisulu and Oliver Tambo. To ensure its implementation, the membership replaced older leaders with a number of younger men. Walter Sisulu, a founding member of the Youth League was elected Secretary-General. The conservative Dr A.B. Xuma, lost the presidency to Dr J.S. Moroka, a man with a reputation for greater militancy. The following year, 1950, Mandela himself was elected to the NEC at national conference.

The ANCYL programme aimed at the attainment of full citizenship, direct parliamentary representation for all South Africans. In policy documents of which Mandela was an important co-author, the ANCYL paid special attention to the redistribution of the land, trade union rights, education and culture. The ANCYL aspired to free and compulsory education for all children, as well as mass education for adults.

When the ANC launched its Campaign for the Defiance of Unjust Laws in 1952, Mandela was elected National Volunteer-in-Chief. The Defiance Campaign was conceived as a mass civil disobedience campaign that would snowball from a core of selected volunteers to involve more and more ordinary people, culminating in mass defiance. Fulfilling his responsibility as Volunteer-in-Chief, Mandela travelled the country, organising resistance to discriminatory legislation. Charged and brought to trial for his role in the campaign, the court found that Mandela and his co-accused had consistently advised their followers to adopt a peaceful course of action and to avoid all violence.

For his part in the Defiance Campaign, Mandela was convicted of contravening the Suppression of Communism Act and given a suspended prison sentence. Shortly after the campaign ended, he was also prohibited from attending gatherings and confined to Johannesburg for six months.

During this period of restrictions, Mandela wrote the attorneys admission examination and was admitted to the profession. He opened a practice in Johannesburg, in partnership with Oliver Tambo. In recognition of his outstanding contribution during the Defiance Campaign Mandela had been elected to the presidency of both the Youth League and the Transvaal region of the ANC at the end of 1952. He thus became a deputy president of the ANC itself.

Of their law practice, Oliver Tambo, ANC National Chairman at the time of his death in April 1993, has written:

To reach our desks each morning Nelson and I ran the gauntlet of patient queues of people overflowing from the chairs in the waiting room into the corridors... To be landless (in South Africa) can be a crime, and weekly we interviewed the delegations of peasants who came to tell us how many generations their families had worked a little piece of land from which they were how being ejected... To live in the wrong area can be a crime... Our buff office files carried thousands of these stories and if, when we started our law partnership, we had not been rebels against apartheid, our experiences in our offices would have remedied the deficiency. We had risen to professional status in our community, but every case in court, every visit to the prisons to interview clients, reminded us of the humiliation and suffering burning into our people.

Nor did their professional status earn Mandela and Tambo any personal immunity from the brutal apartheid laws. They fell foul to the land segregation legislation, and the authorities demanded that they move their practice from the city to the back of beyond, as Mandela later put it, 'miles away from where clients could reach us during working hours.' This was tantamount to asking us to abandon our legal practice, to give up the legal service of our people... No attorney worth his salt would easily agree to do that, said Mandela and the partnership resolved to defy the law.

Nor was the government alone in trying to frustrate Mandela's legal practice. On the grounds of his conviction under the Suppression of Communism Act, the Transvaal Law Society petitioned the Supreme Court to strike him off the roll of attorneys. The petition was refused by Mr. Justice Ramsbottom, finding that Mandela had been moved by a desire to serve his black fellow citizens and nothing he had done showed him to be unworthy to remain in the ranks of an honourable profession.

In 1952, Nelson Mandela was given the responsibility to prepare an organisational plan that would enable the leadership of the movement to maintain dynamic contact with its membership without recourse to public meetings. The objective was to prepare for the contingency of proscription by building up powerful local and regional branches to whom power could be devolved. This was the M-Plan, which was named after him.

During the early fifties Mandela played an important part in leading the resistance to the Western Areas removals and to the introduction of Bantu Education. He also played a significant role in popularising the Freedom Charter, adopted by the Congress of the People in 1955.

In the late fifties, Mandela's attention turned to the struggles against the exploitation of labour, the pass laws, the nascent Bantustan policy, and the segregation of the open universities. Mandela arrived at the conclusion very early on that the Bantustan policy was a political swindle and an economic absurdity. He predicted, with dismal prescience, that ahead there lay a grim programme of mass evictions, political persecutions, and police terror. On the segregation of the universities, Mandela observed that the friendship and inter-racial harmony that is forged through the admixture and association of various racial groups at the mixed universities constitute a direct threat to the policy of apartheid and baasskap, and that it was to remove that threat that the open universities were being closed to black students.

During the whole of the fifties, Mandela was the victim of various forms of repression. He was banned, arrested and imprisoned. For much of the latter half of the decade, he was one of the accused in the mammoth Treason Trial, at great cost to his legal practice and his political work. After the Sharpeville Massacre in 1960, the ANC was outlawed, and Mandela, still on trial, was detained.

The Treason Trial collapsed in 1961 as South Africa was being steered towards the adoption of the republic constitution. With the ANC now illegal the leadership picked up the threads from its underground headquarters. Nelson Mandela emerged at this time as the leading figure in this new phase of struggle. Under the ANC's inspiration, 1,400 delegates came together at an All-in African Conference in Pietermaritzburg during March

1961. Mandela was the keynote speaker. In an electrifying address he challenged the apartheid regime to convene a national convention, representative of all South Africans to thrash out a new constitution based on democratic principles. Failure to comply, he warned, would compel the majority (Blacks) to observe the forthcoming inauguration of the Republic with a mass general strike. He immediately went underground to lead the campaign. Although few answered the call it attracted considerable support throughout the country. The government responded with the largest military mobilisation since the war, and the Republic was born in an atmosphere of fear and apprehension.

Forced to live apart from his family, moving from place to place to evade detection by the government's ubiquitous informers and police spies, Mandela had to adopt a number of disguises. Sometimes dressed as a common labourer, at other times as a chauffeur, his successful evasion of the police earned him the title of the Black Pimpernel. It was during this time that he, together with other leaders of the ANC constituted a new specialised section of the liberation movement, Umkhonto we Sizwe, as an armed nucleus with a view to preparing for armed struggle. At the Rivonia trial, Mandela explained : "At the beginning of June 1961, after long and anxious assessment of the South African situation, I and some colleagues came to the conclusion that as violence in this country was inevitable, it would be wrong and unrealistic for African leaders to continue preaching peace and non-violence at a time when the government met our peaceful demands with force.

He argues: It was only when all else had failed, when all channels of peaceful protest had been barred to us, that the decision was made to embark on violent forms of political struggle, and to form Umkhonto we Sizwe...the Government had left us no other choice.

In 1961 Umkhonto we Sizwe was formed, with Mandela as its Commander-in-Chief. In 1962, Mandela left the country unlawfully and travelled abroad for several months. In Ethiopia he addressed the Conference of the Pan African Freedom Movement of East and Central Africa, and was warmly received by senior political leaders in several countries. During this trip Mandela, anticipating an intensification of the armed struggle, and began to arrange guerrilla training for members of Umkhonto we Sizwe.

Not long after his return to South Africa Mandela was arrested and charged with illegal exit from the country, and incitement to strike.

Since he considered the prosecution a trial of the aspirations of the African people, Mandela decided to conduct his own defence. He applied for the recusal of the magistrate on the ground that in such a prosecution a judiciary controlled entirely by whites was an interested party and therefore could not be impartial, and on the ground that he owed no duty to obey the laws of a white parliament, in which he was not represented.

Mandela prefaced this challenge with the affirmation: "I detest racialism, because I regard it as a barbaric thing, whether it comes from a black man or a white man."

Mandela was convicted and sentenced to five years imprisonment. While serving his sentence he was charged, in the Rivonia Trial, with sabotage. Mandela's statements in court during these trials are classics in the history of the resistance to apartheid, and they have been an inspiration to all who have opposed it. His statement from the dock in the Rivonia Trial ends with these words:

> *I have fought against white domination, and I have fought against black domination. I have cherished the ideal of a democratic and free society in which all persons live together in harmony and with equal opportunities. It is an ideal which I hope to live for and to achieve. But if needs be, it is an ideal for which I am prepared to die.*

Mandela was sentenced to life imprisonment and started his prison years in the notorious Robben Island Prison, a maximum security prison on a small island 7Km off the coast near Cape Town. In April 1984 he was transferred to Pollsmoor Prison in Cape Town and in December 1988 he was moved to the Victor Verster Prison near Paarl from where he was eventually released. While in prison, Mandela flatly rejected offers made by his jailers for remission of sentence in exchange for accepting the bantustan policy by recognising the independence of the Transkei and agreeing to settle there. Again in the 'eighties Mandela rejected an offer of release on condition that he renounce violence. Prisoners cannot enter into contracts. Only free men can negotiate, he said.

Released on 11 February 1990, Mandela plunged wholeheartedly into his life's work, striving to attain the goals he and others had set out almost four decades earlier. In 1991, at the first national conference of the ANC held inside South Africa after being banned for decades, Nelson Mandela was elected President of the ANC while his lifelong friend and colleague, Oliver Tambo, became the organisation's National Chairperson.

Nelson Mandela has never wavered in his devotion to democracy, equality and learning. Despite terrible provocation, he has never answered racism with racism. His life has been an inspiration, in South Africa and throughout the world, to all who are oppressed and deprived, to all who are opposed to oppression and deprivation.

In a life that symbolises the triumph of the human spirit over man's inhumanity to man, Nelson Mandela accepted the 1993 Nobel Peace Prize on behalf of all South Africans who suffered and sacrificed so much to bring peace to our land.

S. Chandrasekhar

$\int$UBRAHMANYAN CHANDRASEKHAR was born into a free-thinking, Tamil-speaking Brahmin family in Lahore, India. He was preceded into the world by two sisters and followed by three brothers and four sisters. His mother Sitalakshmi had only a few years of formal education, in keeping with tradition, and a measure of her intellectual strength can be appreciated from her successful translation of Ibsen and Tolstoy into Tamil. His father C. S. Ayyar was a dynamic individual who rose to the top of the Indian Civil Service. It is not without interest that his paternal uncle Sir C. V. Raman was awarded a Nobel Prize in 1930 for the discovery of the Raman Effect, providing direct demonstration of quantum effects in the scattering of light from molecules.

Education began at home with Sitalakshmi giving instruction in Tamil and English, while C. S. Ayyar taught his children English and arithmetic before departing for work in the morning and upon returning in the evening. The reader is referred to the excellent biography *Chandrasekhar, A Biography of S. Chandrasekhar* (University of Chicago Press, 1991) by Prof. Kameshwar C. Wali for an account of this remarkable family and the course of the third child through his distinguished career in science. Chandrasekhar is the name by which S. Chandrasekhar is universally known throughout the scientific world. Chandrasekhar's life was guided by a dedication to science that carried him out of his native culture to the alien culture of foreign shores. The crosscurrents that he navigated successfully, if not always happily, provide a fascinating tale. He was the foremost theoretical astrophysicist of his time, to paraphrase his own accounting of Sir Arthur Eddington.

The family moved to Madras in 1918 as C. S. Ayyar rose to the position of Deputy Accountant General. Chandrasekhar and his brothers had private tutors then, with Chandrasekhar going to a regular school in 1921. His second year in school introduced algebra and geometry, which so attracted him that he worked his way through the textbooks, the summer before the start of school.

Chandrasekhar entered Presidency College in Madras in 1925, studying physics, mathematics, chemistry, Sanskrit, and English. He found a growing liking for physics and mathematics and an ongoing attraction for English literature. One can assume that his fascination with English literature contributed to his own lucid and impeccable writing style.

Chandrasekhar was inspired by the mathematical accomplishments of S. Ramanujan, who had gone to England and distinguished himself among the distinguished Cambridge mathematicians until his early death in 1920. Chandrasekhar aspired to take mathematics honors, whereas his father saw the Indian Civil Service as the outstanding opportunity for a bright young man. Mathematics seemed poor preparation for the Civil Service. Sitalakshmi supported Chandrasekhar with the philosophy that one does best what one really likes to do. Chandrasekhar compromised with physics honors, which placated his father in view of the outstanding success of Sir C. V. Raman.

On his own initiative Chandrasekhar read Arnold Sommerfeld's book *Atomic Structures and Spectral Lines* and attended lectures in mathematics. His physics professors noticed that he was learning physics largely through independent reading and provided him with the freedom to attend mathematics lectures. In the autumn of 1928, Sommerfeld lectured at Presidency College. Chandrasekhar made it a point to meet Sommerfeld and was taken aback to learn that the old Bohr quantum mechanics, on which Sommerfeld's book was based, was superseded by the wave mechanics of Schroedinger, Heisenberg, Dirac, Pauli, et al., and that the Pauli exclusion principle replaced Boltzmann statistics with Fermi-Dirac statistics. Sommerfeld had already applied the new theory to electrons in metals and kindly provided Chandrasekhar with galley proofs of his paper. Chandrasekhar launched into an intensive study of the new quantum mechanics and statistics and wrote his first professional research paper "The Compton scattering and the new statistics" (1929). In January 1929 he communicated this work to Prof. R. H. Fowler at Cambridge for publication in the *Proceedings of the Royal Society of London.* The name Fowler suggested itself because Fowler had applied the new statistics to collapsed stars (i. e., white dwarfs). Fowler was an open-minded and generous individual who perceived the merit of Chandrasekhar's paper, which he duly communicated to the Royal Society. This contact was to play a crucial role a year later when Chandrasekhar arrived in England.

Heisenberg lectured at Presidency College in October 1929 and Chandrasekhar had the opportunity to carry on extensive discussion with him at the time. Later Meghnad Saha at Allahabad, known for statistical mechanics that provided the interpretation of stellar spectra, invited Chandrasekhar for discussions of Chandrasekhar's paper in the *Proceedings of the Royal Society of London.* Wali, in his biography, contrasts this early appreciation of Chandrasekhar's work by the scientific community with the class snobbery of the British Raj on the personal level.

Final examinations at Presidency College came in March 1930 and Chandrasekhar established a record score. In February, Chandrasekhar was informed that a special Government of India scholarship was to be offered to him to pursue study and research in England for three years. When the scholarship was announced publicly, Chandrasekhar experienced resentment from fellow Indians who perceived him as abandoning his country and his legacy. Worse, it was becoming clear that

Sitalakshmi was terminally ill and, if Chandrasekhar went to England, he would not see her again. True to form Sitalakshmi decided the issue by declaring that Chandrasekhar was born for the world and not just for her.

Chandrasekhar informed the authorities that he wished to use his government scholarship to study and carry on research with R. H. Fowler at Cambridge. The Office of the High Commissioner of India proceeded with the arrangements. Chandrasekhar departed Bombay on July 31, 1930, bound for Venice, from where he travelled by rail to London, arriving on August 19. He undertook the journey in his personal pursuit of science, and that journey was culturally irreversible, a departure from home from which he never really returned.

It is well known that Chandrasekhar spent his time on shipboard working out the statistical mechanics of the degenerate electron gas in white dwarf stars, appreciating, as Fowler had not, that the upper levels of the degenerate electron gas are relativistic. Since it is the upper levels that are affected by changes in density and temperature, it follows that a density change and pressure change p are related by $p/p = 4/3$ rather than the non-relativistic value 5/3 employed earlier by Fowler. The value 4/3 meant that the pressure supporting the star against gravity grows no faster than the increasing gravitational force as the star contracts, with the result that there is a limiting mass above which the internal pressure of the white dwarf cannot support the star against collapse. This is in contrast with the familiar non-relativistic situation where the pressure increases more rapidly than the gravitational forces so that sufficient contraction must ultimately provide a sufficient pressure to block further contraction. The limiting mass was clearly of the order of the mass M. of the Sun (2×10^{33} g). A precise value would require detailed calculations of the interior structure of the star with the precise value of p/p for intermediate levels as well as the upper fully relativistic levels at each radius in the star. But the implication was clear. A massive star, of which there are many, cannot fade out as a white dwarf once its internal energy source is exhausted. Instead it shrinks without limit, always too hot to become completely degenerate, and disappears when the gravitational field above its surface becomes so strong that light cannot escape. In modern language, the massive star eventually becomes a black hole. The reasoning was straightforward and the conclusion was startling. The repercussions that ultimately followed his discovery served to push Chandrasekhar farther into the obscure and lonely byways of science in a foreign Western society and ever more distant from his cultural origins.

Upon arrival in London, Chandrasekhar discovered that the Office of the Director of Public Instruction in Madras and the High Commissioner of India in London had thoroughly bungled his admission to Cambridge. What was more, the secretary for the High Commissioner's Office had not the least interest in correcting the mistake and was openly rude in his assertion of that fact. Chandrasekhar was saved only by the eventual firm intervention of Fowler, who was vacationing in Ireland at the time of Chandrasekhar's arrival in London. The consequences of Chandrasekhar's first research paper were more far reaching than anyone could have imagined.

Chandrasekhar took up his studies at Cambridge and spent a lonely but productive year in intensive study and research. Sitalakshmi died on May 21, 1931, adding grief to his loneliness. Chandrasekhar was introduced to the monthly meetings of the Royal Astronomical Society and became acquainted with E. A. Milne and P. A. M. Dirac. Chandrasekhar devoted his research efforts to calculating opacities and applying his results to the construction of an improved model for the limiting mass of the degenerate star. Milne was enthusiastic about the work, but it turned out later that his enthusiasm was based more on his rivalry with A. S. Eddington than on an appreciation of the scientific merits.

The year of intensive study at Cambridge moved Chandrasekhar to look for a change of scenery, and at the invitation of Max Born he spent the summer of 1931 at Born's Institute at Gottingen. There he became acquainted with Ludwig Biermann, Edward Teller, Leon Brillouin, and Werner Heisenberg. Back at Cambridge in the autumn, Chandrasekhar continued his work on atomic absorption coefficients and mean opacities, but with a growing sense of frustration from his feeling that he was abandoning mathematics through his pursuit of physics and abandoning pure physics through his pursuit of astrophysics. Chandrasekhar was invited to present his results on model stellar photospheres at the January 1932 meeting of the Royal Astronomical Society (RAS) and was complimented by both Milne and Eddington following the presentation.

Chandrasekhar's feeling of frustration with his "peripheral science" led to his spending his third year at Bohr's Institute in Copenhagen. He adapted readily to the informal atmosphere and became acquainted with Victor Weisskopf, Leon Rosenfeld, M. Delbrueck, H. Kopferman, and others. During the time in Copenhagen Chandrasekhar succeeded in convincing himself that his real strength lay in developing and expounding the implications of the basic physical laws of nature as distinct from the pursuit of new laws of nature. He found an interested and appreciative audience in the physics community for his work on degenerate stars. Chandrasekhar was invited to the University of Liege to lecture on his work, following which he was presented with a bronze medal. The overall experience of the year was to ease his mind and set him firmly on a path in theoretical astrophysics.

Chandrasekhar finished the year with four papers on rotating self-gravitating polytropes, which became his Ph.D. thesis. His government scholarship ran out in August 1933 and the question was what to do next. It was clear that there were no opportunities in India unless he rode on the coat-tails of his uncle Raman, which he was loathe to do. Fortunately he won one of the highly competitive appointments as a Fellow of Trinity College, which ran for four years. Milne nominated Chandrasekhar for Fellow of the RAS, and the future was clear for the immediate years at Cambridge. At the monthly meetings in Burlington House Chandrasekhar and such contemporaries as William McCrea generally sat in the back row, but became acquainted with some of the denizens of the front row (e.g., Sir James Jeans, Sir Arthur Eddington, Sir Frank Dyson, and such international visitors as Henry Norris Russell and Harlow Shapley).

Chandrasekhar spent four weeks in the Soviet Union in the summer of 1934 at the invitation of B. P. Gerasimovic, meeting L. D. Landau and V. A. Ambartsumian, along with many other enthusiastic young men. Unhappily only Landau and Ambartsumian survived the massive purges that were soon to follow. Ambartsumian grasped the significance of Chandrasekhar's work on dwarf stars and suggested that it was worth working out exactly (i.e., by direct radial integration of the exact equations, using the complete pressure-density relation). This moved Chandrasekhar to tackle that immense problem upon his return to Cambridge.

The work was accomplished with the aid of a hand calculator and was completed by the end of 1934. He submitted his results for presentation at the January 1935 meeting of the RAS. Eddington had taken an interest in the work through the autumn, often dropping by Chandrasekhar's room to see how things were progressing, but never saying a word to Chandrasekhar about his own private thoughts. Eddington suggested to the secretary of the RAS that Chandrasekhar's work merited double the usual fifteen minutes for presentation and then set himself up to present a paper with the title "Relativistic degeneracy" immediately following. Eddington refused to divulge the nature of his presentation beforehand. McCrea notes in his obituary for Chandrasekhar that Eddington began by pointing out that

Chandrasekhar's calculations were entirely correct based on the relativistic degenerate electron gas. Eddington then noted that the result predicted that a white dwarf with mass in excess of the critical value ($\sim 1.4\ M.$) would continue to radiate and shrink until it disappeared. Then Eddington went on to declare that stars do not behave in that way, and Chandrasekhar's calculations showed only that the theory of relativistic degeneracy is incorrect. Later he asserted that the Pauli exclusion principle does not apply to relativistic electrons. One might have asked Eddington how he knew that stars do not behave in that way, but Eddington was so formidable and influential a person that no one did, apparently. Egos were the same then as now, and one has only to read Eddington's remarkable monograph *Fundamental Theory* (Cambridge University Press, 1944) to realize that he was coming around to the idea that he could deduce the physical nature of the universe from his own personal declarations.

The physicists, Chandrasekhar's young contemporaries (e.g., Pauli, Rosenfeld, Dirac, and others), considered Eddington's assertions to be nonsense, but Eddington moved in a different world. R. H. Fowler and H. N. Russell did not voice the essential points in opposition to Eddington's assertions, evidently intimidated by Eddington's preeminence. Russell, for instance, refused to allow Chandrasekhar to say a few words in response to Eddington's hour long exposition of his personal views at the meeting of the International Astronomical Union (IAU) in Paris in July 1935. Chandrasekhar managed a brief comment at the "International Colloquium on Astrophysics: Novae and White Dwarfs" in Paris in July 1939, but Russell quickly closed the session before a discussion could proceed.

The question of returning to India was raised by C. S. Ayyar, but Chandrasekhar found himself increasingly out of sympathy with the political nature of academia in India. Then Harlow Shapley invited Chandrasekhar to visit the Harvard

Observatory. Chandrasekhar arrived in Boston on December 8, 1935. He enjoyed the friendly atmosphere but was unhappy with the informality after the tightly structured society at Cambridge. He became acquainted with Fred Whipple, Gerard Kuiper, Jerry Mulders, and others. Shapley liked Chandrasekhar's lectures so well that he nominated Chandrasekhar for election to the Harvard Society of Fellows. Then Otto Struve invited Chandrasekhar to visit the Yerkes Observatory of the University of Chicago, followed by an offer of a position as research associate for a year with the expectation that it would become a tenure track appointment in a year. The formal offer came from the office of Chancellor Robert Maynard Hutchins. By the end of the month Chandrasekhar had returned to England.

The Eddington factor had the effect of closing the doors in England, and India offered no acceptable situation. So Chandrasekhar accepted Struve's offer, much to the disgust of his father who saw his son receding farther into the mists of foreign culture.

Since his departure from India in July 1930 Chandrasekhar had corresponded occasionally with Lalitha Doraiswamy who had been a fellow student in physics at Presidency College. She was in Bangalore in 1935 working in Raman's laboratory. They were both aware that they did not know each other very well, and Chandrasekhar had fretted over whether a marriage relationship might interfere with his pursuit of science. Chandrasekhar returned to India for a visit in August 1936 and wrote to Lalitha that he would be at Madras. She took the train to Madras to meet him and his misgivings vanished when they met after six years of geographical separation. They were married September 11, 1936.

Chandrasekhar and Lalitha spent a month in Cambridge on their way to Boston and then the Yerkes Observatory. Struve contacted the legal counsel of the University of Chicago to arrange a visa for Chandrasekhar as a missionary, for otherwise there was no quota for Indians to enter the United States. They arrived at the Yerkes Observatory on Williams Bay on Lake Geneva in Wisconsin on December 21, 1936. They stayed a few days with the Kuipers until their house was ready, and the cold Wisconsin weather was offset by the friendliness of the atmosphere at the observatory.

Lalitha recognized the importance of Chandrasekhar's single-minded pursuit of science, and she supported him at the expense of her own career. She was active in the American Association of University Women and her outgoing sociability complemented Chandrasekhar's more austere view of life so that they got on very well in their new surroundings.

The University of Chicago provided Chandrasekhar with his scientific home for the next fifty-nine years, but there were difficult moments. Chancellor Hutchins intervened on more than one occasion to smooth the way. For instance, in 1938 Struve organized a course in astronomy on the campus of the university to be taught by members of the Yerkes Observatory. However Henry G. Gale, Dean of physical sciences, vetoed Chandrasekhar's participation, evidently on grounds of skin color. When the problem was referred to Hutchins he said, "By all means have Mr. Chandrasekhar teach." At that point it became clear why the original offer of a position had come from the chancellor's office rather than through the Dean.

In 1946 Princeton honored Chandrasekhar by offering him the office and position vacated by the retirement of Henry Norris Russell with a salary approximately double Chandrasekhar's salary at Chicago. Chandrasekhar was inclined to accept. Hutchins matched the Princeton salary and asked Chandrasekhar to come by his office to discuss the matter. In the course of the discussion Hutchins remarked that, if conditions for Chandrasekhar's research were better at Princeton, then he would not attempt to dissuade Chandrasekhar from leaving. When Chandrasekhar responded that he did not think so, Hutchins noted that Chicago could not offer Chandrasekhar the honor of succeeding Henry Norris Russell because Chicago had no Russell. Then he asked Chandrasekhar for the name of the person who had succeeded to Kelvin's chair at the University of Glasgow. Chandrasekhar replied that he had no idea; to which Hutchins replied, "Well, there you are." Chandrasekhar declined the Princeton offer and Hutchins remarked on more than one occasion that acquiring Chandrasekhar for the University of Chicago was one of his major accomplishments as chancellor.

The course of Chandrasekhar's research is perhaps best summarized by the monographs that he wrote as he completed each phase of his work. *An Introduction to the Study of Stellar Structure* (1939) contains his development of the theory of stellar structure, including his work on degenerate stars and the mass limit for white dwarfs, and still makes an excellent textbook on the subject. *The Principles of Stellar Dynamics* (1943) and "Stochastic Problems in Physics and Astronomy" (1943) outline his development of the theory of the dynamics of the motions of stars in the presence of many other stars, showing the frictional drag exerted by neighbouring stars and setting up the basic theory for the evolution of clusters of stars. *Radiative Transfer* (1950) contains his systematic development of the radiative flow of energy in stellar interiors and photospheres including his work on the negative hydrogen ion that dominates the opacity at the surface of a star.

In 1952 the Department of Astronomy revamped its graduate curriculum to keep up with the rapid development in the fields of atomic physics, stellar atmospheres, and stellar evolution. Chandrasekhar had been offering a repertoire of basic courses in stellar structure and radiative transfer. These courses, based in large part on his own fundamental work, provided excellent background for the theoretical students, but were heavy going for the observational students and lacked up-to-date information needed by both groups of students. Chandrasekhar was alienated by the revision and Enrico Fermi seized the opportunity to invite Chandrasekhar to become a member of the Department of Physics and the Institute for Nuclear Studies (now the Enrico Fermi Institute). Chandrasekhar accepted the invitation and henceforth confined his teaching principally to the Department of Physics, commuting from Yerkes to Chicago two days a week to teach. In 1964 Chandrasekhar moved permanently to the Chicago campus, the transition catalyzed by John Simpson's offer of a spacious corner office in the newly constructed Laboratory for Astrophysics and Space Research.

It is ironic that 1952 was also the year Chandrasekhar took up the onerous task of managing editor of the *Astrophysical Journal*. He carried on the responsibilities in his own style, personally attending to the problems of production, refereeing, and politics within the community. The editing was managed with the help of a secretary and an editorial assistant at the University of Chicago Press. Under Chandrasekhar's leadership the journal developed into the leading international journal in astrophysics. The journal was in reality privately owned by the University of Chicago. Chandrasekhar was its heart and soul, and Chandrasekhar realized the unstable character of the situation. In 1967, he set in motion a reorganization that would transfer the primary responsibility to the American Astronomical Society (AAS), although the actual production was to continue at the University of Chicago Press. The rapid expansion of the journal from six issues a year to two large issues a month made it increasingly difficult for a single editor to handle, particularly with Chandrasekhar's establishment of the *Astrophysical Journal Letters* in 1967. So Chandrasekhar proposed that there be associate editors to assist the managing editor. To make a long story short, the new order of things was approved by the American Astronomical Society, and Chandrasekhar was able to pass on his enormous burden to the new team in 1971. It is remarkable that during his years as editor Chandrasekhar carried on his scientific research at a rate not noticeably diminished at the same time that he taught his quota of courses in the Department of Physics. It is an example of the extraordinary feats that can be accomplished through dedication and self-discipline to the exclusion of nearly everything else in one's life. His retirement from the position as editor was a great relief to Chandrasekhar. He had never intended that the burden should have continued for so long.

Chandrasekhar and Lalitha were faced with the question of U.S. citizenship, and after thinking about it for a time came to the conclusion that it was the only realistic choice. It was a big step away from their origins, but to do otherwise would have ignored the fact of their permanent commitment to a life in the United States. So in 1953 they became naturalized citizens. Lalitha's careful explanation of the evolution of their thinking did little to assuage the bitter feelings of C. S. Ayyar who saw the move only as a betrayal of their cultural origins rather than an inevitable evolution in their circumstances. Following citizenship Chandrasekhar was elected to the National Academy of Sciences in 1955.

During Chandrasekhar's early years as editor, the field of plasma physics and the confinement of ionized gas in magnetic fields in the laboratory was coming into prominence, with the hope, still unrealized today, of producing available power through the fusion of hydrogen into helium. At the same time it was being appreciated that the physics of fully ionized gases (i.e., plasmas) is the basis for the dynamical behavior of stellar interiors, atmospheres, and the interstellar gas. Plasma conditions range all the way from the tenuous, essentially collisionless gases in space to the incredibly dense plasma in the central regions of a star. Chandrasekhar was attracted by the challenge of the unknown. He expounded the existing theory of collisionless plasma in a course on the foundations of plasma physics based on the standard free-particle approach and the collisionless Boltzmann equation. S. K. Trehan put together a book *Plasma Physics* (University of Chicago Press, 1960) based on the notes from that course. In collaboration with A. N. Kaufman and K. M. Watson, Chandrasekhar carried through the immense calculation of the dynamical stability of the collisionless plasma confined in an axial magnetic field. At the same time Chandrasekhar entered into an extensive study of the dynamical stability of fluids in various configurations, including the presence of magnetic fields and rotation of the entire system. His contributions are summarized in his monograph *Hydrodynamic and Hydromagnetic Stability* (1961).

From there Chandrasekhar took up the classical and unfinished problem of the dynamics of rotating, self-gravitating spheroids of homogeneous incompressible fluids. The problem had been initiated by Newton in connection with the oblateness of Earth and carried on from there by such great names as Maclaurin, Reimann, Dedekind, Jacobi, Dirichlet, et al. Chandrasekhar reopened the unfinished problems with the tensor virial equations whose great power had not been appreciated up to that time. The results of that work appear in his monograph *Ellipsoidal Figures of Equilibrium* (1969).

The work on self-gravitating objects soon brought Chandrasekhar to the doorstep of general relativity as the basic theory of gravity. His efforts in that field led to the development of the Chandrasekhar-Friedman-Schultz instability, which became a source of gravitational radiation from black holes. Extensive investigation of the Kerr metric and the rotating black hole led to the monograph *The Mathematical Theory of Black Holes* (1983). Chandrasekhar also developed the post-Newtonian approximation for treating the field equations of general relativity. It is now the means for calculating the gravitational radiation from multiple star systems, etc. He went on to work out a variety of exact solutions to the equations of general relativity in collaboration with B. C. Xanthopoulos and V. Ferrari, showing some of the remarkable singularities that turn up in the interaction of gravitational waves and at the apex of the conical space solutions. One of the more curious discoveries was that the radial pulsations of a star, which are known from Newtonian gravitation to exhibit overstability in the presence of dissipation (e.g., viscosity) become unstable in general relativity through the energy loss represented by the emission of gravitational waves. Thus the star without internal dissipation is stable according to Newtonian theory, but unstable in the context of general relativity.

As a brief aside it is interesting to note that in 1982 Chandrasekhar was invited to lecture on Sir Arthur Eddington at the celebration at Cambridge of the hundredth anniversary of his birth. The lectures are published in the small book *Eddington, the Most Distinguished Astrophysicist of His Time* (1983). The lectures emphasize the remarkable insights of Eddington into stellar structure and his early recognition of the implications of Einstein's general relativity. Chandrasekhar's reflections on Eddington's assertions on electron degeneracy and the Pauli exclusion principle are of particular interest.

By 1990 Chandrasekhar had developed a growing interest and admiration for the work of Sir Isaac Newton, and over the next several years he constructed a detailed and critical review of Newton's *Principia.* The results of this effort are published as *Newton's Principia for the Common Reader* (1995). This was the first time that a world class physicist undertook a thorough reading and critical commentary of the *Principia,* dispelling such perpetuated notions that Newton's theory of the perturbations of the orbit of the Moon is in error, or that some of his diagrams were incorrectly drawn.

Chandrasekhar's book *Truth and Beauty* (1987) shows an entirely different side of his thinking. It includes his Ryerson

Lecture "Shakespeare, Newton, and Beethoven" in which he explored and compared the motivations and feelings involved in the creation of science and art.

Chandrasekhar's scientific papers are collected in seven volumes under the title *Selected Papers, S. Chandrasekhar* (1989-96). They complement the monographs listed above and provide a more detailed historical picture of the day-by-day development of his thinking.

Chandrasekhar attached great importance to training Ph.D. students. He saw them clearly as the future of astrophysics when the present generation of working scientists has passed into retirement and beyond. Struve had assigned him the responsibility for the weekly colloquium, held on Monday afternoons, and Chandrasekhar saw to it that the graduate students were in regular attendance. The Yerkes faculty, graduate students, and visitors presented their work at appropriate times, and Chandrasekhar gave each hundredth colloquium himself, as well as many in between. The count of weekly colloquia passed 500 before Chandrasekhar moved to the campus. He also conducted seminars on Monday evenings for the edification of the graduate students, who took turns reporting on interesting papers that had appeared in the literature. Chandrasekhar supervised forty-six known Ph.D. research students, many of whom have become prominent in the field of astrophysics, and not a few of whom are members of the National Academy of Sciences. Chandrasekhar was a stern taskmaster who insisted on rigorous training and research. The graduate courses in theoretical astrophysics taught at Yerkes by Chandrasekhar were the usual preparation, until the early fifties. After that most of Chandrasekhar's students came through the Department of Physics. Once a student successfully completed the Ph.D., Chandrasekhar gave his full support in getting the student established in the scientific community. In fact Chandrasekhar's support was not limited to his students alone. He appeared at critical moments in the career of this writer, as with others as well.

It is no surprise, of course, to learn that Chandrasekhar was awarded many honorary degrees and medals. He was elected a fellow of the Royal Society in 1944, which awarded him the Bruce Medal in 1952. The Royal Astronomical Society awarded him its Gold Medal in 1953. He was awarded the National Medal of Science by President Lyndon Johnson in 1967. The fundamental nature of Chandrasekhar's mass limit to degenerate stars has come to be appreciated in the astronomy and physics communities, recognizing that it is perhaps the most direct and striking example of the effect of quantum physics on macroscopic bodies. Chandrasekhar was awarded a Nobel Prize by King Carl Gustav in 1983 in recognition of his work of fifty years before. On the other hand it must be appreciated that Chandrasekhar's work on radiative transfer, stellar dynamics, dynamical stability of fluids, plasmas and self-gravitating bodies, and gravitational theory collectively represent a much larger contribution to physics and astrophysics than the more spectacular mass limit.

Chandrasekhar's death in 1995 heralded the end of the era that developed the basic physics of the star. He was the most prolific and wide ranging of those who applied hard physics to astronomical problems.

Albert Einstein

Albert Einstein was born at Ulm, in Württemberg, Germany, on March 14, 1879. Six weeks later the family moved to Munich and he began his schooling there at the Luitpold Gymnasium. Later, they moved to Italy and Albert continued his education at Aarau, Switzerland and in 1896 he entered the Swiss Federal Polytechnic School in Zurich to be trained as a teacher in physics and mathematics. In 1901, the year he gained his diploma, he acquired Swiss citizenship and, as he was unable to find a teaching post, he accepted a position as technical assistant in the Swiss Patent Office. In 1905 he obtained his doctor's degree.

During his stay at the Patent Office, and in his spare time, he produced much of his remarkable work and in 1908 he was appointed Privatdozent in Berne. In 1909 he became Professor Extraordinary at Zurich and in 1911 Professor of Theoretical Physics at Prague. Returned to Zurich in the following year to fill a similar post. In 1914 he was appointed Director of the Kaiser Wilhelm Physical Institute and Professor in the University of Berlin. He became a German citizen in 1914 and remained in Berlin until 1933 when he renounced his citizenship for political reasons and emigrated to America to take the position of Professor of Theoretical Physics at Princeton. He became a United States citizen in 1940 and retired from his post in 1945.

After World War II, Einstein was a leading figure in the World Government Movement, he was offered the Presidency of the State of Israel, which he declined, and he collaborated with Dr. Chaim Weizmann in establishing the Hebrew University of Jerusalem.

Einstein always appeared to have a clear view of the problems of physics and the determination to solve them. He had a strategy of his own and was able to visualize the main stages on the way to his goal. He regarded his major achievements as mere stepping-stones for the next advance.

At the start of his scientific work, Einstein realized the inadequacies of Newtonian mechanics and his special theory of relativity stemmed from an attempt to reconcile the laws of mechanics with the laws of the electromagnetic field. He dealt with classical problems of statistical mechanics and problems in which they were merged with quantum theory: this led to an explanation of the Brownian movement of molecules. He investigated the thermal properties of light with a low radiation density and his observations laid the foundation of the photon theory of light.

In his early days in Berlin, Einstein postulated that the correct interpretation of the special theory of relativity must also furnish a theory of gravitation and in 1916 he published his paper on the general theory of relativity. During this time he also contributed to the problems of the theory of radiation and statistical mechanics.

In the 1920's, Einstein embarked on the construction of unified field theories, although he continued to work on the probabilistic interpretation of quantum theory, and he persevered with this work in America. He contributed to statistical mechanics by his development of the quantum theory of a monatomic gas and he has also accomplished valuable work in connection with atomic transition probabilities and relativistic cosmology.

After his retirement he continued to work towards the unification of the basic concepts of physics, taking the opposite approach, geometrisation, to the majority of physicists.

Einstein's researches are, of course, well chronicled and his more important works include *Special Theory of Relativity* (1905), *Relativity* (English translations, 1920 and 1950), *General*

Theory of Relativity (1916), *Investigations on Theory of Brownian Movement* (1926), and *The Evolution of Physics* (1938). Among his non-scientific works, *About Zionism* (1930), *Why War?* (1933), *My Philosophy* (1934), and *Out of My Later Years* (1950) are perhaps the most important.

Albert Einstein received honorary doctorate degrees in science, medicine and philosophy from many European and American universities. During the 1920's he lectured in Europe, America and the Far East and he was awarded Fellowships or Memberships of all the leading scientific academies throughout the world. He gained numerous awards in recognition of his work, including the Copley Medal of the Royal Society of London in 1925, and the Franklin Medal of the Franklin Institute in 1935.

Einstein's gifts inevitably resulted in his dwelling much in intellectual solitude and, for relaxation, music played an important part in his life. He married Mileva Maric in 1903 and they had a daughter and two sons; their marriage was dissolved in 1919 and in the same year he married his cousin, Elsa Löwenthal, who died in 1936. He died on April 18, 1955 at Princeton, New Jersey.

C. V. Raman

Chandrasekhar **Venkata Raman** was born at Tiruchirapalli in Southern India on November 7th, 1888. His father was a lecturer in mathematics and physics so from the beginning he was immersed in an academic atmosphere. He entered Presidency College, Madras, in 1902, and in 1904 passed his B.A. examination, winning the first place and the gold medal in physics; in 1907 he gained his M.A. degree, obtaining the highest distinctions.

His earliest researches in optics and acoustics - the two fields of investigation to which he had dedicated his entire career- were carried out while he was a student.

Since at that time a scientific career did not appear to present the best possibilities, Raman joined the Indian Finance Department in 1907. Though the duties of his office took most of his time, Raman found opportunities for carrying on experimental research in the laboratory of the Indian Association for the Cultivation of Science at Calcutta (of which he became Honorary Secretary in 1919).

In 1917 he was offered the newly endowed Palit Chair of Physics at Calcutta University, and decided to accept it. After 15 years at Calcutta he became Professor at the Indian Institute of Science at Bangalore (1933-1948), and since 1948 he became Director of the Raman Institute of Research at Bangalore which was established and endowed by himself. He also founded the *Indian Journal of Physics* in 1926, of which he was the Editor. Raman sponsored the establishment of the Indian Academy of Sciences and has served as President since its inception. He also initiated the *Proceedings* of that academy, in which much of his work has been published, and was President of the Current Science Association, Bangalore, which publishes *Current Science (India)*.

Some of Raman's early memoirs appeared as Bulletins in the *Indian Association for the Cultivation of Science* (Bull. 6 and 11, dealing with the "Maintenance of Vibrations"; Bull. 15, 1918, dealing with the theory of the musical instruments of the violin family). He contributed an article on the theory of musical instruments to the 8th Volume of the *Handbuch der Physik*, 1928. In 1922 he published his work on "Molecular Diffraction of Light", the first of a series of investigations with his collaborators which ultimately led to his discovery, on the 28th of February, 1928, of the radiation effect which bears his name ("A new radiation", *Indian J. Phys.*, 2 (1928) 387), and which gained him the 1930 Nobel Prize in Physics.

Other investigations carried out by Raman were: his experimental and theoretical studies on the diffraction of light by acoustic waves of ultrasonic and hypersonic frequencies (published 1934-1942), and those on the effects produced by X-rays on infrared vibrations in crystals exposed to ordinary light. In 1948, Raman through studying the spectroscopic behaviour of crystals approached in a new manner fundamental problems of crystal dynamics. His laboratory has been dealing with the structure and properties of diamond and the structure and optical behaviour of numerous iridescent substances (labradorite, pearly felspar, agate, opal, and pearls).

His other interests have been the optics of colloids, electrical and magnetic anisotropy, and the physiology of human vision.

Raman has been honoured with a large number of honorary doctorates and memberships of scientific societies. He was elected a Fellow of the Royal Society early in his career (1924), and was knighted in 1929.

Alexander Fleming

Alexander Fleming was born in a remote, rural part of Scotland. The seventh of eight siblings and half-siblings, his family worked on 800-acre farm a mile from his house. The Fleming children spent most of their time exploring streams, valleys, and moors of the countryside. "We unconsciously learned a great deal from nature," said Fleming.

When their father died, Fleming's eldest brother inherited the farm. Another brother Tom had studied medicine and was opening a clinic in London. Soon, four Fleming brothers and a sister were living together in London. Alec, as he was called, had moved to London when he was about 14, and went to the Polytechnic School in Regent Street. Tom encouraged him to enter business. After completing school he was employed by a shipping firm, though he did not much like it. In 1900, when the Boer War broke out between the United Kingdom and its colonies in southern Africa, Alec and two of his brothers joined a Scottish regiment. This turned out to be as much a sporting club as anything; they honed their shooting, swimming, and even waterpolo skills, but never went to the Transvaal. Soon after this, the Flemings' uncle died and left them each 250 pounds. Tom's medical practice was now thriving and he encouraged Alec to put his legacy toward the study of medicine.

Fleming took top scores in the qualifying examinations, and had his choice of medical schools. He lived equally close to three different schools, and knowing little about them, chose St. Mary's because he had played waterpolo against them. In 1905 he found himself specializing as a surgeon for almost random a reason. His switch to bacteriology was even more surprising. If he took a position as a surgeon, he would have to leave St. Mary's. The captain of St. Mary's rifle club knew that he was desperate to improve his team. Knowing that Fleming was a great shot he did all he could to keep him at St. Mary's. He worked in the Inoculation Service and he convinced Fleming to join his department in order to work with its brilliant director — and to join the rifle club. Fleming would stay at St. Mary's for the rest of his career.

In 1909 German chemist-physician Paul Ehrlich developed a chemical treatment for syphilis. He had tried hundreds of compounds, and the six hundred and sixth worked. It was named salvarsan (meaning "that which saves by arsenic"). The only previous treatments for this disease had been so toxic as to often kill the patient. Ehrlich brought news of his treatment to London, where Fleming became one of the few physicians to administer salvarsan. He did so with the new and difficult technique of intravenous injection. He soon developed such a busy practice he got the nickname "Private 606."

When World War I broke out, most of the staff of the bacteriology lab went to France to set up a battlefield hospital lab. Here they encountered infections so drastic that soldiers quickly died from them. Yet they were still simple infections. Fleming felt there must be something, a chemical like salvarsan, that could help fight microbe infection even in wounds caused by exploding shells. During the course of the war, Fleming made many innovations in treatment of the wounded, but this was soon overshadowed by the work he did afterwards.

Back in St. Mary's lab in the 1920s, Fleming searched for an effective antiseptic. He discovered lysozyme, an enzyme occurring in many body fluids, such as tears. It had a natural antibacterial effect, but not against the strongest infectious agents. Fleming had so much going on in his lab that it was often in a jumble. This disorder proved very fortunate. In 1928 he was straightening up a pile of Petri dishes where he had been growing bacteria, which piled in the sink. He opened each one and examined it before tossing it into the cleansing solution. One made him stop and say, "That's funny." Some mould was growing on one of the dishes — not too unusual — but all around the mould, the staph bacteria had been killed — very unusual. He took a sample of the mould. He found that it was from the penicillium family, later specified as penicillium notatum. Fleming presented his findings in 1929, but it raised little interest. He published a report on penicillin and its potential uses in the British Journal of Experimental Pathology. Fleming worked with the mould for some time, but refining and growing it was a difficult process better suited to chemists. The work was taken over by a team of chemists and mould specialists, but was cut short when several of them died or relocated. It took World War II to revitalize interest in penicillin, and Howard Florey and Ernst Chain picked up the work.

In recognition for his contribution, Alexander Fleming was knighted in 1944. With Chain and Florey he was awarded the Nobel Prize in 1945.